THE
AMERICAN ELECTORAL COLLEGE

The
American Electoral College

By

Roger Lea MacBride

The Caxton Printers, Ltd.
Caldwell, Idaho
1953

Printed and bound in the United States of America by
The CAXTON PRINTERS, Ltd.,
Caldwell, Idaho
74641

To
MY FATHER AND MOTHER

FOREWORD

I wrote this book because I was curious. Two members of Congress—Senator Lodge of Massachusetts and Representative Gossett of Texas—had introduced a joint resolution to amend the Constitution of the United States. The gravamen of their proposed amendment was the abolition of the present method of choosing the President of the United States and the substitution of a modified popular election system.

Now, I am one of those mossbacks who think that no change ought to be made in the fundamental mechanics of American government without detailed study of all the probable and possible consequences. And this proposal seemed to me to call for a major change. So, I started to look over material on the procedures of presidential elections. I was astonished to find that no complete study had been made since 1906. There was nowhere available a concise summary of the pros and cons of either the Lodge-Gossett amendment or of the Coudert amendment, which is an alternative plan now being considered by Congress. Consequently I undertook to search out the facts and the arguments and make them available.

Why did the Founding Fathers select a system of presidential electors to choose the head of the executive branch of the Federal government? How did they intend that system to function? To find the answer to these questions seemed the logical first step in an analysis of the problem. The first chapter is therefore devoted to an account of events at the Constitutional Convention of 1787. Did the Electoral College fail in its purpose, and if so, why? Chapter Two seeks an answer. Should either of the proposals currently before Congress be adopted? I have treated these questions through an historical and analytical approach in subsequent chapters.

The system of presidential electors who gather in an assembly, or college, quadrennially, has had a profound effect upon the political institutions of this country. I have tried to deal in some detail with these effects in order to come to a solution which will at once meet the defects of present usage and retain its benefits.

I wish to thank Mr. J. Harvie Williams for his explanation of the means and purposes of the Coudert plan. Mr. L. Myron Scher also aided me. I am particularly anxious to acknowledge gratefully the continuing inspiration and assistance given me by Mrs. Rose Wilder Lane.

R. L. M.

Chappaqua, New York
June, 1952

TABLE OF CONTENTS

THE
AMERICAN ELECTORAL COLLEGE

CHAPTER ONE

"This subject has greatly divided the House, and will also divide people out of doors. It is in truth the most difficult of all on which we have had to decide."[1] So spoke one of the most astute members of the Federal Convention in 1787, and to his statement there was no dissent. It was, of course, to the method of electing the President of the United States that he referred.

Picture a group of men attempting that which had never been tried before—the conscious creation of a government. Imagine these men—for the most part the most respected and intelligent in their colonies—selected for this momentous task by the legislatures and governors of the several states. Sincerely patriotic, the members of the Convention were desperately anxious to create a government as close to the ideal as possible. Undoubtedly influenced by personal considerations and by regional considerations, their object on the whole was nevertheless to secure an equitable, workable, and just government. They met in Philadelphia, on May 25, and were to remain in session until early September to accomplish this task.

The number of problems with which the authors of the Constitution had to deal were mind-staggering, and the problem of picking a means of choosing a head of state was not the least of these. I have taken this account of the deliberations from the only full and authoritative account of the Convention, Madison's

Journal, with occasional reference to the sketchy official journal published by Congress thirty years later.

On the twenty-ninth of May Edmund Randolph of Virginia laid before the Convention a rough plan for a Federal Constitution. Part of it suggested that a national executive of an unstated number of persons should be elected for an unstated number of years by the national legislature. On the same day, Mr. Charles Pinckney of South Carolina offered a plan proposing a single executive, but not specifying mode of election or length of service.

On June 1, when the Convention reached a discussion of this section of the proposals, James Wilson of Pennsylvania, later a Justice of the United States Supreme Court, voiced his wish that however chimerical the possibility of its adoption might be, the executive be elected by the people. Thus he would be as independent as possible from the states. And on the following day he offered this alternative to the Randolph proposal:

> ... the executive magistracy shall be elected in the following manner: That the States shall be divided into—districts and that the persons qualified to vote in each district for members of the first branch of the National Legislature elect—members for their respective districts to be electors of the executive magistracy; that the said electors of the executive magistracy meet at—and they, or any—of them, so met, shall proceed to elect by ballot, but not out of their own body,—person—in whom the executive authority of the National Government shall be vested.[2]

He urged this plan as a compromise between popular election and election by the national legislature, which would promote greater confidence in the executive than would be the case if the latter plan prevailed.

Elbridge Gerry of Massachusetts then spoke up,

agreeing that election by the legislature would be a mistake, since corruption and intrigue would undoubtedly be common. But he felt that Mr. Wilson's plan was premature in superseding the authority of the states, and urged that a suffrage of the states be taken. Also he doubted that the people ought to act directly in the choice of Electors, being ignorant of personal characters in large districts.

On the taking of a vote, Mr. Wilson's substitute was defeated by a vote of eight states to two, and election by the national legislature approved by a like vote.[3] The Convention moved on to other business. On the ninth, however, Mr. Gerry moved to reconsider the question, and it was so voted. Upon this approval, he advanced the suggestion that the executive be selected by the state executives, with voting power equal to their representation in the legislature. He summarized objections to the mode which the Convention had adopted: (1) It would lessen the executive's independence of the legislature; (2) It would give birth to intrigue before the election; (3) It would give rise to partiality on the part of the executive towards his supporters after the election. Mr. Gerry's counter, on the other hand, would avoid these difficulties while offering the best chance of selecting the most fit men. Randolph immediately rose to his feet and protested the inadequacy of Gerry's plan. Not only would the state executives be little conversant with the men of other states, he said, but the smaller states would lose all hope of electing an executive. Further, the executive so chosen would not be likely to defend the national rights against state encroachments. Shortly thereafter, Mr. Gerry's plan was defeated ten to one.[4]

On Friday the fifteenth of June, Mr. Patterson laid

before the Convention what has been since termed the New Jersey Plan, in many respects differing from the Randolph suggestions as they had been modified by the Convention; however, the section concerning the election of the executive again supported the legislative election. The Convention proceeded to take up its recommendations in order, and it was not until the seventeenth of July that they came to that clause. It precipitated the sharpest debate upon the subject yet.

Gouverneur Morris (Pa.) : The Executive, if elected by the legislature, will be its mere creature, whereas, if elected by the people at large, some man of continental reputation will be chosen, in spite of the difficulties of this mode of election.

Roger Sherman (Conn.) : The people at large, besides never being sufficiently informed to make a proper choice, will never give a majority to any one man. They will be likely to vote for a man from their own state, thus giving the largest state a distinct advantage in the matter of choice.

James Wilson (Pa.) : A concurrence of a majority is not a necessary principle of election; but if it were, the legislature might make a choice where no candidate received a majority of the votes. This at least would restrain the choice to a good nomination, and prevent to a great degree intrigue and cabal.

Charles Pinckney (S.C.) : In a popular election, the largest states by combining could carry their candidates. The Legislature, on the other hand, would be most interested in securing an executive who would properly carry their laws into execution.

Gouverneur Morris : It is said that the people will be led by a few designing men. Although it might happen in a small district, it cannot happen throughout the continent. Nor will the people be uninformed of the illustrious men who have merited their confidence. Election by the Legislature will result in executive dependence, and consequently in Legislative usurpation and tyranny, as happened in England in the last century.

George Mason (Va.) : It would be as unnatural to refer the choice of a proper Chief Magistrate to the people as it would to refer the trial of colors to a blind man. The Legislature,

16

which we are entrusting with many duties, should be expected to perform this one properly.

James Wilson: The legislature might deserve confidence in some respects and distrust in others. This branch of business was the most corruptly managed of any that had been committed to legislative bodies.

Hugh Williamson (N.C.) : The largest State, in a popular election, will be sure to succeed. . . . As the Convention has decided that the executive will be ineligible for reelection [this decision was, of course, later changed] there will be less chance of his dependence upon the legislature.[5]

The question of election by the people was moved, and it was beaten, 9-1. The question of election by Electors chosen by the state legislatures was moved, and beaten, 8-2. The question of election by the national legislature was moved, and was unanimously carried.[6]

Only two days later, the Convention returned to the subject. Debate had been carried on concerning the length of the executive's term, and the desirability of his eligibility for re-election. The delegates, according to James Wilson, began to feel that if the executive were twice eligible he should not be chosen by the legislature.[7]

James Madison took up the argument. He asserted that if it were a fundamental principle of free government that the legislative, executive, and judicial powers should be *separately* exercised, it was equally so that they be *independently* exercised. Therefore the election of the executive should be made by a source such that he would have a free agency with the legislature. Even if he were not subject to re-election, election by the legislature would not meet this condition. He would favor an election by the people, who would vote for some citizen of merit who had attracted general esteem, did not the problem of suffrage in the South make

17

improbable the establishment of that method. Therefore, he urged the method liable to the fewest objection,
the substitution of Electors. After some further debate, including an attempt by Mr. Gerry to resubmit
his plan, the question was taken. The question "Shall
the National Executive be appointed by Electors?" was
affirmed, 6-3, and the question "Shall the Electors be
chosen by the State Legislatures?" passed 8-2.[8] The
Convention then approved a motion by Mr. Gerry establishing a preliminary apportionment of Electors among
the states, and postponed a consideration of the permanent ratios.

But on July 24 the Convention reversed its last decision. On the motion of New Jersey's William Houston
the election of the executive was restored to the national
legislature. It was urged that gratitude or favoritism
would be felt by the elected candidate as much toward
Electors as members of the legislature, and the former
would not be men of the character of the latter.

Two of the great men of the session, James Madison
and Colonel Mason, rose in the following two days and
spoke at length with the object of clarifying the issue.

Madison opened by stating that the election must be
made by some existing national or state authority, by a
special authority derived from the people, or by the
people themselves. With reference to the national government, he assumed that the only conceivable source
of an election would be the legislature. That agency, he
felt, was liable to several insuperable objections. In the
first place, the election would influence unduly the later
conduct of the executive. Second, the election would
agitate and divide both the legislature and the public.
Third, intrigue between the candidates and members
of the legislature would unquestionably take place with

18

great frequency. Fourth, foreign powers would spare no pains or expense to secure an American executive, limited though his powers might be, favorable to their hemispheric interests. In the states, the available sources of election are the legislatures and the executives. He had many objections to the first method, supreme among which was the strong likelihood that they would select a man who would not strongly oppose encroachment upon the national government by the respective states. The state executives, being standing bodies, would be subject to intrigue by candidates, their friends, and foreign powers.

The option, therefore, lies between an election by Electors as a special agency and the people. The former has many advantages, and the Electors, chosen for the occasion and meeting at once, would be little subject to cabal or corruption. An election by the qualified part of the people he liked best, but would not repeat all of the arguments for it. The objection that the larger states would have undue influence he admitted, but minimized its importance in the future. And as a Southerner, he was prepared to make the sacrifice entailed by the disproportion of qualified voters in the North and South, since local considerations must give way to the general interest.[9]

Colonel Mason proceeded to detail the various proposals advanced and reject them in turn. Popular election he described as "an act which ought to be performed by those who know the most of eminent characters and qualifications, . . . not performed by those who know least." Mr. Gerry asserted in the same vein that the principle of popular election would be radically vicious: one set of men, dispersed through the nation, might influence the appointment by deluding the people.

He added that since enough had been said against election by state legislatures and executives, and inasmuch as selection by a body of special Electors had been finally rejected, he would not argue against these proposals. He concluded, therefore, that election by the legislature was the only practicable expedient.[10] It was confirmed again shortly after he concluded.

On August 6 the Committee on Detail reported out a draft of a constitution drawn from the previous debates and presentations. When the section dealing with the election of the President arose, an extremely significant point was raised. What if the two Houses of Congress should disagree on the choice of a President? Either one house would be overridden by the pressure of the necessity of making a choice, or the deadlock would continue indefinitely with catastrophic consequences. The difficulty was somewhat smoothed over by changing the wording to provide election by the joint houses of Congress, but the Convention members from the smaller states were definitely uneasy about the drop in influence of their Senators. When Mr. Morris inevitably moved that the election be given over from the legislature to electors, the question lost by a tie vote of 4-4, with two states divided and two absent.[11]

At the end of August the weary Convention gave into the hands of a Grand Committee of Eleven, headed by Roger Sherman, all of the postponed and disputed parts of the Constitution, in order that they might be cast into the most generally acceptable form. On the fourth of September this committee offered the following alteration in the method of election of the President (as it was now decided the Chief Executive would be called):

He shall hold his office during the term of four years, and together with the Vice President, chosen for the same term, shall be elected in the following manner, viz: Each State shall appoint, in such manner as its Legislature may direct, a number of Electors equal to the whole number of Senators and members of the House of Representatives to which the State may be entitled in the Legislature. The Electors shall meet in their respective States, and vote by ballot for two persons, one of whom at least shall not be an inhabitant of the same State as themselves; . . . [here follow details of the transmission of results to the national legislature]. The person having the greatest number of votes shall be the President, if such number be a majority of that of the Electors; and if there be more than one who have such a majority, and have an equal number of votes, the Senate shall immediately choose by ballot one of them for President; but if no person has a majority, then from the five highest on the list, the Senate shall choose by ballot the President; and in every case after the choice of the President, the person having the greatest number of votes shall be Vice President; but if there remain two or more who have equal votes, the Senate shall choose from them the Vice President. The Legislature may determine the time of choosing and assembling the Electors, and the manner of certifying and transmitting their votes.[12]

As no little surprise was manifested by several members of the Convention as to the reasons for the sudden change in the previously determined manner of election, Mr. Gouverneur Morris felt obliged to summarize them. (1) The danger of intrigue and faction if the appointment were made by the legislature. (2) The inconvenience of the necessity of rendering the executive ineligible a second time if he were so elected. (3) The difficulty of establishing a court of impeachments, other than the Senate. Mr. Morris had earlier warned that since a power to impeach is essential, it is an additional argument against election by the legislature, of which the Senate which will try the impeachment, is a part.[13] (4) No one was satisfied with the legislative

21

method. (5) Many were even anxious for an immediate choice by the people. (6) The indispensable necessity of making the executive independent of the legislature.

Mr. Pinckney was angered by the change. He rapped out his objections to the plan: (1) it would throw, in most elections, the choice of the President to the Senate; (2) the Electors would be strangers to the candidates and unable to decide on their merits; (3) the executive was made re-eligible, thus endangering the public liberty; (4) the same men who in fact elected the President would be his judges in the case of impeachment.

To the implied charge that corruption might be equally prominent in the event of a Senate election as in a legislative election as previously decided upon, Mr. Wilson answered that it "would not open cabal anew, as . . . if the election be made as it ought, as soon as the votes of the Electors are opened, and it is known that no one has a majority of the whole, there can be little danger of corruption."[14] The question was postponed until the following day, when the discussion swung into the final phase, preparatory to settling the matter for all time.

The opponents of the plan for an Electoral College found argument after argument beaten down or ignored, and centered upon, as a last effort, the supposition that the election would nearly always be thrown into the Senate. Mr. Morris disposed of this contention to the satisfaction of most of the Convention by arguing that as each Elector is to give two votes, more than one fourth will give a majority. As one vote must be given to a man outside the Elector's state, this vote will not be thrown away and will fall on generally known men. And if a President has given satisfaction, the Electors will choose him again without recourse to the Senate; if the President is disliked, the Electors will give their votes with care to an opposition candidate, that the incumbent might not be re-elected.

The Great Debate, for such it was, was over. On September 6 the Constitutional Convention by a vote of 9-2, with only the Carolinas opposed, and New York (represented solely by the ever-absent Alexander Hamilton) not recorded, approved the principle of election of the President by a body created specially for that purpose. During the next day many minor changes were made in the wording of the article, which we may have occasion to mention later. (See Appendix A for the final text.) One deserves attention here: in the event that a ballot of Electors failed to choose a President, it was decided that the House of Representatives, voting by states, should select him, while the Senate should choose the Vice President. In so deciding the Convention maintained the basis of the great compromise—equal representation of the states in the Senate, and popular representation in the House— which enabled the states to unite. The House was selected as the agency to make an ultimate choice, if needful, partly as a concession to those who wanted the election closer to the voters, and partly to avoid giving to the already powerful Senate an additional power.

The struggle over the method of choosing the head of state was not a bitter battle between men of conflicting ideologies. Most of them had been students of the theories of Locke and Hume, and not a few had read Adam Smith's recent book *The Wealth of Nations*. The participants in the debate desired to achieve the same goal: a state which would secure, and not encroach

23

upon, the liberty of the citizen. They sought earnestly to come on common ground as to the means best adapted to this end. It was because they saw in the Chief Executive, a necessary officer of state, a person who might become a tyrannical king-and-prime-minister if the opportunity arose, that they were so very anxious to avoid a method of selecting him which might increase this possibility.

At the outset, the election method most had supposed would be the natural choice was demonstrated to be surrounded with danger. The delegates were firmly convinced that the executive, judicial, and legislative departments must not only be separated, but set against each other in certain ways in order that the growth of a too-powerful state might be prevented. As the debate continued it became clear to the convention's members that apart from the "cabal and corruption" which there was every reason to expect would be present in a legislative election of a President, the elected man would in most cases be far from separate from the legislature. Some feared that a strong legislature would impose its will on the executive, and some feared that the supporters of the elected candidate would form a dominant clique in the legislature, following the executive wherever he led. In either case, the two departments would not in fact be separate; in no case could the executive be completely independent of the body that elected him. The inevitability of such a situation doomed the plan.

Objection-free alternatives, however, were not easy to find. The suggestion that various authorities in the states elect the President were not popular. Governors were eliminated as a body of men too liable to corruption. State legislatures, meeting and voting separately, would constitute an agency too awkward to

24

consider. The opinion of such men as Madison and Wilson, that the qualified voters ought to elect the President directly, was not generally held. The difficulty of equating the voting strength of the slave-holding South with that of the populous North, and the conviction that Americans in the collective ought not to exercise that power *directly* (". . . democracies have ever been spectacles of turbulence and contention, have ever been found incompatible with personal security and the rights of property, and have in general been as short in their lives as they have been violent in their deaths"[15]) eliminated it from the running as a possibility even before the Convention opened.

It was James Wilson who proposed the compromise in the first week, although it was not taken seriously until later. In its eventual form, the idea of a College of Electors was satisfactory to nearly every delegate: they felt that they had accomplished an important task in achieving a suitable method of election.[16] To it attached none of the objections offered to the other plans. The Electors would be selected for one task alone, which they would proceed promptly to perform. Thus the danger of corruption was minimized. As agents of the people, they would presumably be no less meritorious citizens than those other officials elected by the voters. Deliberating on the men who were best qualified for the presidency, they would make a choice at least equal and in all probability superior to that which could be effected by any other agency. The composition of the College, in another brilliant stroke, was set at precisely that of the joint houses of Congress. Thus the Electors formed an alternate legislature, as able in every way to select a President as the actual Congress, but subject to none of the disabilities con-

25

nected to the latter. In the event that it did not reach a choice, the election was to return to the House, a popularly elected body operating in this one case as a Federal body.

In its ability to analyze a situation, dispose of undesirable solutions, and select a compromise acceptable to nearly all, while violating none of the fundamental principles around which the new government was to be shaped, the Constitutional Convention has never been surpassed. And I think it is unquestionable that the establishment of the Electoral College was among the most brilliant of its achievements.

CHAPTER TWO

The electoral system as envisaged by its authors and the electoral system in practice were, as will develop in this chapter, two different things. The Founders were not indifferent to the existence of personal or political factions: most of them had encountered them in their own states. Some were even leaders of distinct political groups. The electoral system (the meeting of whose members came to be called a college rather than a congress or convention to distinguish it from other American political institutions) designed as it was to deprive both Congress and the voters of total power over the election[1] could only fulfill its purpose if these factions did not develop into tight-knit national organizations, and it was with the hope that such a situation would not come to pass that the members of the Convention watched its operation during the first elections.

Of course everyone knew that George Washington would be the unanimous choice for President no matter what the method of election. He himself said: "If I should conceive myself in a manner constrained to accept, I call Heaven to witness that this very act would be the greatest sacrifice of my personal feelings and wishes that ever I have been called upon to make."[2] He was constrained to accept, and so the real contest for the first two elections was that of the vice-presidency. In 1789 party spirit did not really exist; indeed, it had scarcely had time to come into being between the ratification by an effective number of states and the selection of Electors. John Adams was elected to the vice-presidency with little determined opposition.

Since time was so short, most of the states undertook to appoint the Electors by legislative action. A few, however, including Pennsylvania, Maryland, and Virginia, provided for popular election, which took place "without great excitement."[3] No uniform method of choosing the Electors was considered. Insofar as some of the states looked to the future, they based their decisions regarding future methods of choosing them on widely varying grounds. Some officials raised their eyebrows at the mere suggestion that the citizenry should elect the Electors; some assumed that that would be the case as a matter of course.

By the end of Washington's second administration party spirit reached a degree of bitterness which, according to Stanwood, was not surpassed for a century.[4] It is not here our purpose to trace the details of that clash between organized groups: it will be enough to say that it grew out of two philosophies for the most part fundamentally opposed on the nature and power of the Federal government, and it centered around two or three personalities. On the one hand stood Alexander Hamilton and the Vice-President of the United States, John Adams; on the other stood Thomas Jefferson. The election of 1796 was between the last two named, and it resulted in an Adams victory. Electors were chosen in that year by the people in six states, and by legislatures in ten states, and in every case the Electors were picked as men *pledged* to one candidate or the other.

It was perhaps one of the cruelest acts of fate that

events so developed in the first decade of the Republic, as far as the electoral system was concerned. It was natural and to be expected that divisions of thought would occur from time to time throughout the nation on such questions as the proper relationship of the national and state governments, and on particular policies to be followed, but a deep, two-way cleavage of thought with popular leaders of each faction bred disaster for the electoral system. Issues were subordinated to a considerable extent to the merits of the candidates, and in a very few years the two became inseparable: the candidate *made* the issues. Electors then became mere tools of the agency which elected them, whether that agency was the legislature or the "popular will," chosen duly to record a vicarious presidential vote. This status of presidential Electors was partly confirmed by the Supreme Court of the United States in April, 1952. It held in the case of *Ray* v. *Blair* that if the local party organization requires an oath from candidates for elector that they will support the nominee of the national party, the Constitution of the United States does not require the local party to allow candidates who refuse to take the oath to run on the party ticket in a primary election.

The function which presidential Electors were intended to perform was eliminated. From this time onward Electors almost never exercised independent judgement.[5]

The Electoral College thus died before it was mature. It never had an opportunity of selecting a President in the way intended. In the first two elections the members did not need to make a decision. In every subsequent election the decision was made for them, and eventually no man was chosen for the job unless

29

he were certain to conform to the dictates of the party.[6] Before a great period of time had passed, many of the more astute thinkers of the republic had recognized this fact. These men divided into at least two groups: those who wished to abolish the form to conform to substance, and those who wished to return to (or create) substance matching the form. Their recommendations will be discussed in the following two chapters.

One would naturally suppose that changing the function (or disconnecting) of a portion of a precisely geared machine (as the national government was designed to be) would lead to unexpected and probably undesirable results. And that was what happened. The remainder of this chapter will be devoted chiefly to the development of the Electoral College as a group of mechanical men, to the difficulties which resulted in the electing of Presidents, and to the attempts to solve the difficulties.

As I have mentioned, party feeling developed strongly in the last decade of the eighteenth century. Fairly formal groupings of Federalists and Anti-Federalists existed by 1800 in every state. How the tickets were formed is a matter of conjecture.[7] It is, nevertheless, a fact that everyone knew that Jefferson and Burr were being backed by the Anti-Federalists for the presidency and vice-presidency, respectively, and Adams and Pinckney by the Federalists. When the Electors met, they dutifully cast their votes for the chosen men.[8] It was with some astonishment that the nation learned that the election would have to go to the House, since Jefferson and Burr were tied with more than a majority of the whole number of Electors voting for them; and it was with bitterness that the Jeffersonians learned that Burr and the Federalists had joined hands in an attempt to capture the presidency. The balloting took a week, with no choice effected in thirty-five tries. Finally Hamilton persuaded several Federalists to cast blank votes in order to allow Jefferson's election, and what had been shaping up as a very serious crisis was averted.

What had happened? It was perfectly plain to most people that a man intended to be Vice-President had made a bold attempt to secure the top office. But the answer to the question lies deeper than that. Clearly, the party system had pulled a boner. Burr had been chosen to run with Jefferson because he was politically powerful in New York, which was a state not only among the nation's largest and electorally most important, but also in the North and thus balanced against Mr. Jefferson's Virginia. It is probable that few people outside his own circle wanted him to be President—and if the Electors had voted according to their own convictions he would never have been a real contender for the job. But the Electors voted for the ticket, as they had been expected to, and the strain on the machinery produced a warped product. The Electors were originally created to vote for the two finest men they could find for the job; in that way, ties were not to be expected—but if they occurred, it was supposed that there would be little difference in the qualifications of the tied candidates. But the machinery had not changed by 1800—only the conception of it had. Men intended for different posts in the government were voted for equally, with a deadlock ensuing that few had foreseen and none wanted.

Obviously, something had to be changed. And it was before the next election. An amendment to the Constitution (See Appendix A for text) was passed by Congress and ratified by the requisite number of states before 1804. It provided, simply, that the President and the Vice-President would be voted for *separately* by the Electors. The trouble had been removed, it was thought, and little further attention was paid to the Electors as a nationally functioning group.

During the first three decades of the new century the states chose the Electors in varying ways. Most of them had made provision for a popular election after the first elections, but a few (including South Carolina, which continued the practice until the Civil War[9]) chose by legislature. Among the states electing by popular vote, two methods were current. In some the entire group of Electors to which the state was entitled was selected by the majority of the voters throughout the state. This system was called the general ticket method. In other states the Electors were chosen in Congressional (or other) districts, and the result in one district did not effect the others in any way. The Senatorial Electors were chosen at large, by the other Electors, or special districts were created for them. Thus, to choose a convenient election for illustrative purposes,[10] in the Jackson-Clay election of 1832 the state of New Jersey, operating under the general ticket method, voted 23,856 to 23,393 for Jackson. As a result, Jackson got eight electoral votes, Clay none. In Maryland, however, where the district system had been in use for many years, the Electors were divided five for Clay and three for Jackson, although the votes of almost as many citizens were even more evenly divided on the whole—19,156 for Jackson and 19,160 for his opponent.

The political leaders of the time, however, were becoming more aware of the potentialities of the electoral system. It became more and more obvious that a state which could deliver its entire electoral vote to a candidate was politically more powerful than one whose vote was likely to be split.[11] Consequently the legislature began to drop the district system in state after state, substituting the general ticket. The four-cornered election of 1824 insured the death of the district system. Even though the states employing the system cast most of their votes for one candidate, the *effective* vote was reduced by an appreciable margin. Maryland, for example, had given only eighteen effective votes during the years 1796-1812 inclusive, although in the latter alone six Electors voted.[12] It was clear to the party men that a situation might arise at the next election, or in the near future, in which the undivided vote of their state might be decisive; consequently, the number of districted states dropped to four in 1828, one in 1832, and none thereafter.[13] The Electoral College was now adapted as nearly as it could be to the national party system at that time being firmly cemented as a fixture in American elections.

It was the election of 1824 that laid the foundation for the new parties[14]—the Federalists having died some years before. That contest depended almost entirely upon personalities, but after the results were known Jackson's disappointed followers resolved into a distinct group. In time they became known as Democrats. The opposition, which really developed as a cohesive force after the 1836 election, was first known as National Republican, and later as Whig.

The 1836 election provides an interesting example of the way in which the general ticket electoral system could be used to defeat a popular candidate or party. In that year the Democrats nominated Martin Van

33

Buren at the behest of retiring President Jackson. It was clear to all that only a political miracle could prevent his accession to the presidency. Consequently, "The Opposition wisely determined not to attempt a concentration of their strength, but to take advantage of all elements of local hostility to the administration, in the hope of throwing the election into the House of Representatives."[15] General Harrison was a candidate of the formal opposition, Judge White was expected to capture Tennessee and Georgia, Daniel Webster was nominated and voted for by Massachusetts, and South Carolina could be counted upon to throw its votes to someone unconnected with the Administration. "The scheme was a promising one"[16] but it failed. Even though the entire vote of the opposition states could be delivered, the Democrats controlled a majority of the Electors.[17] An interesting occurrence in this election was the failure of the Democratic vice-presidential candidate to secure a majority of votes. The election was made by the Senate, which without great excitement chose him on the first ballot. It was the only time the Senate ever performed this task.

Two other elections deserve mention. In 1860 a President was elected even though Electors favorable to him were not on the ballot in nine out of thirty-three states, and even though the opposition polled 66 per cent of the popular vote in the nation—a greater percentage than F. D. Roosevelt received at the height of his popularity.[18] The Southern states had warned that if this man—Abraham Lincoln—were chosen,. they would leave the Union, and they kept that promise. Had the district system been in use, no President, it is likely, would have been chosen by the Electors, and the election would have devolved upon the House, where

34

a President might have been chosen who could have averted a secession.[19]

The Hayes-Tilden contest of 1876 probably aroused more comment than any other political event of the nineteenth and twentieth centuries. After election day nearly every newspaper announced that Tilden, the Democrat, had secured a majority of the popular and electoral votes.[20] Republican headquarters, however, announced that Hayes was elected by one electoral vote.[21] This position was based on double returns from four states—three carpetbag Southern states, and Oregon. An electoral commission was created by Congress to decide which set of votes from each of the states was valid, with the provision that its decision was final in each case, unless both Houses of Congress overrode it. The commission was composed of eight Republicans and seven Democrats—a composition, need it be said, which was not anticipated by the Tilden supporters. It is not necessary to go into the very complicated details of the settlement here. The G.O.P. depended upon the successful defense of every one of their claims for victory; the Democrats needed only one electoral vote. By a straight party vote the commission supported every G.O.P. claim, and by a straight party vote the Republican Senate upheld, and the Democratic House rejected, its decisions. Hayes was declared elected with a count of 185 to 184.

Feverish passions were aroused during the conduct of the inquiry. David Dudley Field, the famous lawyer, burst into print with a treatise concerning the correct method for Congress to follow in determining the result.[22] Horatio Seymour, a former Democratic candidate for the presidency, said: "The glory of this centennial year thus fades away and darkens into this

35

national shame and reproach. Aroused patriotism can crush resistance to law, but corruption kills honor, virtue, and patriotism, saps the foundations of society and brings down the structure of states and nations in ruin and dishonor."[23] And yet these same virtuous Democrats attempted to purchase one—any—Republican Elector at almost any price, in order to make certain a "fair" election result![24] After the immediate turmoil had died down, agitation from several sources for a change in the electoral system sprung up anew. The recommendations will be discussed in the next chapter.

The significance of the 1876 election concerns not so much the Electoral College as the extent to which the votes submitted to Congress as valid electoral votes may be counted or not counted at its discretion. Clearly, if Congress or any agency it designates (such as the electoral commission of 1876) has an absolute right to reject electoral votes, the power to elect really lies with it. On the other hand, if it has no such power, there can be no protection against fraudulent electoral votes from that source.

Two years after the disputed election a most comprehensive survey of the Electoral College was published by David McKnight. In it he sought to find an answer to this dilemma. His findings are most clearly expressed by means of two quotations from his work: "The question is as to the constitutionality of the power of official counting and canvassing by Congress. Are they the [constitutionally] expressed powers of Congress? They are not. Are they properly incidental to any of the expressed powers of Congress? They certainly are not. Therefore, Congress cannot exercise them. The law is clear and specific; it neither enlarges any power of Congress nor grants them a new power. And the principle here involved is applicable to any and every claim which Congress can advance to the right of canvassing the electoral votes . . . the technical, legal, and natural construction of the language of the Constitution demonstrates the investiture of the President of the Senate with the power of canvassing and counting the votes."[25]

McKnight here denied the validity of the practice of the past: that Congress might determine the status of a vote by majority action. In contending that Congress does not have this power, he applied a strict interpretation of the Constitution.

To deny Congress the ability to do more than watch the President of the Senate count eliminates the very grave danger that a hotly partisan Congress may some day count its candidate in on specious grounds. This danger may have seemed more real in 1878 than today, but that it exists cannot be denied. There lies, however, a danger in the reverse direction: can a false count by a mistaken or corrupt President of the Senate be remedied? McKnight answers: "On a given day the President of the Senate opens the certificates, thus disclosing the legal votes according to the law or Constitution, and declares the result. It is the work of a few hours only, and there can be no failure in it. With an efficient law, if any State be dissatisfied with her representation, the case can be laid before the courts of the United States, and be by them determined before the arrival of the Fourth of March. Everything is done by the Law, as was intended, justice is meted out, and peace and order inevitably follow."[26]

In short, then, Mr. McKnight maintained that Congress does not possess the power to decide the validity

37

or invalidity of electoral votes, both because of the specific wording of the Constitution and because the Founders intended to prevent the interposition of that body in the election.[27] The power and duty to do so is lodged solely in the President of the Senate, and any recourse from his decision must be taken through the courts (presumably Congress would request the Supreme Court to hear the case immediately). This contention is fully backed by both history and logic, and if it prevails in the future, will prevent a repetition of the 1876 debacle.

It was in that election that the American system of electing its Chief Executive reached its final form. It took a short eighty-seven years for the Electoral College to become a vestigial appendage: save for the influence it has exerted on the type of presidential and vice-presidential candidates and the form of campaigning (to be discussed later) it might as well not have existed during the last three-quarters of a century.

The national factions centering around popular and respected men destroyed the independence of thought which should have characterized the Electoral College. The dependence of thought brought about an unexpected and undesired crisis at the turn of the century. The possibility of its recurrence in the future was obviated by a technical amendment to the Constitution. That amendment served to further confirm the parties, as they became known, by enabling them to offer the electorate two candidates with balanced strengths. The Electors' continued dependence upon the parties caused the abandonment of the district system of election in favor of the general ticket method. When that became the universal practice, no state could afford to change to the district system, and the chance that the Electors

38

would be able to reassert independence was hopelessly gone. Finally, Congress overstepped the bounds of constitutional authority in the latter part of the century in order to choose between rival electoral votes. It declared one set of men elected to the presidency and vice-presidency, and when it did that, all pretense vanished that the provision so proudly incorporated into the Constitution by the Federal Convention was being obeyed. The Electoral College had become a hindrance to the proper choice of a President.

CHAPTER THREE

Though the Electoral College had become worthless, belief in its importance had been so strong that it was incorporated in virtually unchanged form into the new Constitution of the Confederate States of America in 1861.[1] That belief had not been held by all men, however. Both before and after the Civil War there were reformers: those who wished to do away with the Electors more or less completely, substituting another method of presidential election, and those who wished to alter the operation of the system in order to restore to it a measure of its original purpose. This chapter will discuss fully the first type.

Advocates of a popular election of the President were by no means absent from the historical scene. There were several in the Constitutional Convention, and they appeared from time to time thereafter, growing in strength. One of the most energetic was Senator Benton of Missouri, whose twenty-year effort to bring about a change began in 1823. His bill provided roughly that the Electoral College would be abolished, and that the people of the states would vote in uniform districts for the President. Each district would have a "vote" for the President, which would be decided without the influence of other districts. If no majority was received, the election, as before, would be decided by the House of Representatives. In support of his plan he said that it would give to each portion of the Union its due share in the electing of a President, as well as being agreeable to the Constitution's intention, then being violated by the general-ticket system, "to give to each mass of persons entitled to one elector the power of giving an electoral vote to any candidate they preferred."[2] His suggestion was put aside for that session of Congress, but a committee was created to study it and make a recommendation. It did so in early 1826. The proposal was much like the Benton plan, with the exception of a provision which called for a runoff election if no candidate received an electoral majority. This addition both eliminated the need for a House election—which had so recently proved disastrous to the proposers of this amendment, the Crawford and Jackson men—and obviated "all excuses for caucuses and conventions to concentrate public opinion."[3]

President Jackson, understandably, firmly opposed the institution of Electors and the resort to a House election when the Electoral College failed to make a choice. In his first message to Congress he urged strongly that the Benton proposal be adopted, and he continued to ask for a change in his next six addresses. Premising that the Electors should follow popular desire, he said ". . . in proportion as agents to execute the will of the people are multiplied, there is danger of their wishes being frustrated; some may be unfaithful, all are liable to err."[4] Neither the Benton nor any similar plan was adopted, however; Dougherty, a student of the problem, says "it was too radical and it was not in consonance with the evolution of party government."[5]

In the 1870's discussion of the electoral system again was popular in Congress. In 1874 Senator Oliver P.

41

Morton introduced a proposed amendment containing most of the features of the original Benton bill, but adding that the two Senatorial "votes" were to be awarded to the candidates with the highest popular vote in the state.[6] Of course, the election of 1876 led to a plethora of proposals when the dust had settled. The plans were all of one type in that they called for popular election in effect, but they differed in the manner of achieving this end. Some, like the plan of Mr. Cravens of Arkansas, would have retained the fiction of an electoral vote, but would have divided it in accordance with party strength within the state. Some, like Finlay of Ohio, supported an out-and-out popular election, with a plurality to win.[7]

In May of 1878 a committee of the House chosen to report a suitable plan offered a suggestion which has been taken up again more recently. It would dispense with the Electors, the citizens voting directly for President and Vice-President. The states would possess "presidential votes" equal in number to their former Electors, and these would be multiplied by each candidate's popular vote, and the result divided by the whole popular vote. The resulting fractions would be added by the two Houses of Congress, and the candidate with the highest number would be declared winner. The plan did not come on to the floor of the House for discussion.[8]

The current interest in the Electoral College began with the efforts of Representative Lea of California. In both 1930 and 1932 he succeeded in obtaining a hearing for his proposed bill before the House Committee on Election of President, Vice-President, and Representatives in Congress, but it was never, insofar as I have been able to discover, brought to a vote in either

House. His plan was very similar to that offered by Cravens after the Tilden defeat. It provided, simply enough, that the electoral vote—to be a fictitious quantity equal to the former Electors—be divided among the candidates for President in accordance with their popular vote, and that the man with the highest electoral vote was to be President.

Instead of discussing at length the merits and demerits of Representative Lea's proposal as they were brought out in the record of those years, I shall proceed at once to a thorough investigation of the latest in the long line of popular-vote plans: the Lodge-Gossett amendment. The Lodge-Gossett plan resembles the earlier Lea amendment closely, as does the testimony concerning it. It would be useless to repeat arguments and confusing to separate them. With the idea of conveying a clear and precise understanding of the only plan of its type likely to be adopted at present, therefore, it would be wise to consider it exhaustively.

Representative Ed Gossett is a Democrat from Texas; Senator Henry Cabot Lodge is a Republican from Massachusetts. They introduced the same bill (see Appendix A for the full text) into the two Houses of Congress, and in 1949 hearings were held by subcommittees of the Judiciary committees of both Houses. The material which follows is taken largely from the printed reports of those hearings.[9]

The Lodge-Gossett amendment provides that the qualified voters in each state shall vote directly for the presidential candidate of their choice. An official of the state sends to the president of the U.S. Senate a list of the votes each candidate received in his state. Then the exact proportion of each state's fictitious electoral vote is allotted to the candidates in accordance with their popular votes. Computations will not be carried beyond thousandths of one vote unless doing so would change the result of the election. The candidate who receives the highest number of electoral votes is elected, whether or not his total is a majority.

In order to simplify the process of following the arguments, I have summarized and compacted the testimony given by many witnesses. The most important supporters of the proposed amendment were the two authors and former Representative Lea. The most telling arguments against it were delivered by Basil Brewer, a Massachusetts newspaper publisher, assisted by G.O.P. Senator Ferguson. These are the six major arguments advanced in behalf of the Lodge-Gossett amendment:

1. Under the present system, it is possible for a candidate to receive a minority of the popular vote, and yet secure a majority of the electoral vote. The proposed amendment would virtually end all chance of this undemocratic possibility.[10]

2. Under the present system, some voters for the presidency are disfranchised. Those who vote for a candidate who loses in a particular state are not counted in the final returns. Since the entire electoral vote of the state is awarded to the man with the most votes, the votes of those who opposed him are actually credited to him. Former Representative Lea said: "I know of no legitimate reason why every candidate should not receive credit for all votes cast for him. Those are just basic requirements of a just system of election."[11]

3. The amendment will tend to break up the "solid" or one-party states in the South. Because a Republican vote will count even in a strongly Democratic state,

44

every effort will be made to bring as many voters to the polls as possible.[12]

4. Absolutely democratic elections will be achieved through the counting of every vote. Further, abolition of the Electoral College will insure a choice: "One very important feature of the electoral system is that it shall be so designed that it will always result in the selection of one of the candidates. It is far better to have a system that will definitely produce such a result under a fair system of counting votes than it is to throw the election into a decision of any small group of men such as Congress...."[13]

5. Existing provisions concerning the choice of Electors, the manner in which their vote is cast and counted, and the deciding of elections in Congress is open to fraud. To the extent that Electors have come to express the will of the people, they are useless. But while they are useless, they may be also dangerous if they seek to exert their vote in a legally correct but morally wrong way. In a close election an Elector may be bought. Further, acts of God may prevent the casting of the electoral vote in the proper way, so that it may be invalid. Further, an election in Congress is fraught with possibilities for an unfortunate outcome. The election of 1824, in the House, elevated a minority candidate to the presidency. The proposed amendment does away with these causes of difficulties. There will be no Electors to miscast their votes, and there will be no House election. Tie votes will be impossible: the election will be decided in November.[14]

6. The general-ticket system of choosing Electors followed now restricts national campaigns to a few large pivotal states. Since a candidate who can carry

45

all of the six or seven largest states is certain of election, and a candidate who can carry a majority of them is almost certain, no candidate can afford to spread his time and money thinly. He must concentrate on those states.[15] The Lodge-Gossett amendment will eliminate the necessity of concentrating all efforts on the large states, and with it will eliminate these evil consequences of the present system:

a. Citizens outside these states are deprived of the educational value of a campaign directed toward them, and their concern with national affairs is correspondingly lessened. Under the new system campaigns would be conducted throughout the U.S.[16]

b. Domination of the large states is secured by small but organized minorities, who are able to virtually dictate terms to the major parties for their support. In a close election, such groups are able to swing the state. The result is morally degrading promises made by the politicians to these groups —promises which are usually at variance with the well-being of the general public. The FEPC plank adopted in 1948 by both parties was offered by Representative Gossett as an example, among others. The new system would eliminate the need to "swing a state" to get any electoral votes, and thus minimize the dependence of the major parties on minor groups for support in one state.[17]

c. At present presidential candidates are picked from a restricted field: the large states. Obviously, a few votes in one of the largest states may sway it in the right direction, in a close election. Therefore a man must be picked who is thought

46

to be popular in the major states, particularly New York. In the years since the Civil War, no Southerner and only one Westerner—Hoover—has been elected President. By reducing the relative importance of the most populous states, the field of selection will be widened: surely so important an office should be filled by a man at least equal to other contenders with regard to the state from which he comes.[18]

Perhaps the best method of arriving at a clear understanding of the Lodge-Gossett bill will be to outline the arguments proposed against it in the same sequence as those for it. With the exception of the general claims of point number six above, each assertion made by the proponents of the bill has been cogently attacked, and insofar as it is possible, each refutation will be numbered similarly.

1. It is urged that under the present system a candidate can receive a minority of the popular vote and yet be elected President with an electoral majority. The first thing that might be said is that this state of affairs should not disturb Lodge-Gossett supporters, who contemplate the at least occasional election of a plurality —and hence a minority—candidate.

Secondly, it is not only possible but extremely probable that a candidate might receive a majority of the popular vote and yet a minority of the electoral vote. A simple example was provided by an opponent of the Lodge amendment.

Take two states each having 24 electoral votes, and assume that 4 million popular votes are cast in one, 2.4 million in the other. In state A the Republican receives $3/4$ of the popular vote, the Democrat $1/4$; in state B the Republican receives $1/8$, the Democrat $7/8$. The popular vote in the two states together is 3.3 million for the Republican, 3.1 million for the Democrat. But under the Lodge amendment—which provides for prorating the electoral votes of each state between the candidates in proportion to the popular votes therein—the Democrat is credited with 27 electoral votes to the Republican's 21.[19]

Or, more elaborately, take the case of 1948, in order to compare the chart prepared by Senator Lodge (see Table I) for that year with a possible sequence of events. Assume that in that year Thurmond's votes had gone to Truman, as they normally would have (this same analysis holds for all of the Roosevelt elections in which the South was solid). Then:

Had Thurmond's vote gone to Truman in 1948, Governor Dewey, under the Lodge plan, would have been 66 electoral votes behind Truman in the 11 states of the Solid South— Truman 11, State electoral vote 96, Dewey 11, State electoral vote 30.

Obviously, with Truman 66 electoral votes ahead in the South, Dewey must be 67 votes ahead in the remaining 37 states in the North to win, making the necessary Dewey 37-State electoral vote 236 against Truman's 168.

To secure 236 electoral votes in the 37 States of the North and win over Truman, Mr. Dewey must, on the average, secure 24,924,768 popular votes to 17,742,984 for President Truman, a popular vote lead in 37 States of 7,181,784.

The average popular vote per electoral vote in the 37 States of the North and center of the country in 1948 was 105,613, compared with a popular vote average of 37,300 per electoral vote in the 11 States of the South.

In securing 96 electoral votes in the South, including the Thurmond total, President Truman's popular vote would have been 3,580,800; Dewey's 30 electoral votes would have represented 1,119,000 popular votes, for a Truman plurality in the 11 States of the South of 2,461,800 popular votes.

Dewey's 37-State plurality, as shown, was 7,181,784. His net plurality, to win the election, would have to be then 4,719,984 in the country as a whole.[20]

TABLE I
The Presidential elections of 1948

State	Popular vote in thousands Rep.	Dem.	Electoral vote present system Rep.	Dem.	Electoral vote Lodge-Gossett Rep.	Dem.
Alabama	41	......	......	......	2.0	......
Arizona	77	95	......	4	1.8	2.1
Arkansas	51	149	......	9	1.9	5.6
California	1,895	1,913	......	25	11.8	11.9
Colorado	239	267	......	6	2.8	3.1
Connecticut	437	423	8	......	4.0	3.8
Delaware	69	67	3	......	1.5	1.5
Florida	194	281	......	8	2.7	3.9
Georgia	76	254	......	12	2.2	7.3
Idaho	101	107	......	4	1.9	2.0
Illinois	1,961	1,994	......	28	13.8	14.0
Indiana	821	807	13	......	6.4	6.3
Iowa	494	522	......	10	4.8	5.0
Kansas	423	351	8	......	4.3	3.6
Kentucky	341	466	......	11	4.6	6.2
Louisiana	72	136	......	......	1.7	3.3
Maine	150	111	5	......	2.8	2.1
Maryland	294	286	8	......	4.0	3.8
Massachusetts	909	1,151	......	16	6.9	8.8
Michigan	1,038	1,003	19	......	9.3	9.0
Minnesota	483	692	......	11	4.4	6.3
Mississippi	5	19	......	......	.2	.9
Missouri	655	917	......	15	6.2	8.7
Montana	96	114	......	4	1.7	2.1
Nebraska	264	224	6	......	3.3	2.7
Nevada	29	31	......	3	1.4	1.5
New Hampshire	121	107	4	......	2.1	1.4
New Jersey	981	845	16	......	8.0	7.3
New Mexico	80	105	......	4	1.1	2.2
New York	2,841	2,780	47	......	21.6	21.2
North Carolina	258	459	......	14	4.6	8.1
North Dakota	115	95	4	......	2.1	1.7
Ohio	1,445	1,452	......	25	12.3	12.4
Oklahoma	268	452	......	10	3.7	6.3
Oregon	260	243	6	......	3.0	2.8
Pennsylvania	1,902	1,752	35	......	17.8	16.4
Rhode Island	134	188	......	4	1.7	2.3
South Carolina	5	34	......	......	.3	1.9
South Dakota	129	117	4	......	2.1	1.9
Tennessee	203	270	......	11	4.4	5.9
Texas	282	750	......	23	5.7	15.0
Utah	124	149	......	4	1.8	2.2
Vermont	75	45	3	......	1.8	1.1
Virginia	172	200	......	11	4.5	5.3
Washington	386	476	......	8	3.4	4.2
West Virginia	316	429	......	8	3.4	4.6
Wisconsin	590	647	......	12	5.6	6.1
Wyoming	47	52	......	3	1.4	1.5
TOTAL	21,969	24,105	189	303	221.4	257.8

TABLE I (Continued)

State	Popular vote in thousands		Electoral vote present system		Electoral vote Lodge-Gossett	
	S.R.	Prog.	S.R.	Prog.	S.R.	Prog.
Alabama	171	1	11	......	8.8	.1
Arizona	......	3	......	......	......	.1
Arkansas	40	......	......	......	1.5	......
California	1	190	......	......	......	1.2
Colorado	......	6	......	......	......	.1
Connecticut	......	13	......	......	......	.1
Delaware	......	1	......	......	......	......
Florida	89	11	......	......	1.2	.2
Georgia	85	1	......	......	2.4	......
Idaho	......	4	......	......	......	.1
Illinois	......	......	......	......	......	......
Indiana	......	9	......	......	......	.1
Iowa	......	12	......	......	......	.1
Kansas	......	4	......	......	......	......
Kentucky	10	1	......	......	.1	......
Louisiana	204	3	10	......	4.9	.1
Maine	......	1	......	......	......	......
Maryland	2	10	......	......	......	.1
Massachusetts	......	38	......	......	......	.3
Michigan	......	46	......	......	......	.4
Minnesota	......	27	......	......	......	.3
Mississippi	167	......	9	......	7.8	......
Missouri	......	4	......	......	......	......
Montana	......	7	......	......	......	.1
Nebraska	......	......	......	......	......	......
Nevada	......	1	......	......	......	.1
New Hampshire	......	2	......	......	......	......
New Jersey	......	42	......	......	......	.4
New Mexico	......	......	......	......	......	......
New York	......	509	......	......	......	.7
North Carolina	69	3	......	......	1.2	.1
North Dakota	......	8	......	......	......	.2
Ohio	......	37	......	......	......	.3
Oklahoma	......	......	......	......	......	......
Oregon	......	15	......	......	......	.2
Pennsylvania	......	55	......	......	......	.5
Rhode Island	......	2	......	......	......	......
South Carolina	102	......	8	......	5.8	......
South Dakota	......	2	......	......	......	......
Tennessee	73	1	1	......	1.6	......
Texas	107	3	......	......	2.1	.1
Utah	......	2	......	......	......	......
Vermont	......	2	......	......	......	......
Virginia	43	2	......	......	1.1	.1
Washington	......	31	......	......	......	.3
West Virginia	......	3	......	......	......	......
Wisconsin	......	25	......	......	......	.2
Wyoming	......	1	......	......	......	......
TOTAL	1,169	1,156	39	......	38.5	9.8

Source: House Hearing on H. J. Res. 2, 81st Cong., pp. 44-45.

It is obvious that if Dewey's Northern plurality in this case were only 4,600,984, he would have dropped the majority of electoral votes to Mr. Truman while gaining a majority of the popular votes.

To cite another, historically more clear, example: in 1900, William McKinley was elected over William J. Bryan with the biggest popular plurality ever recorded up to that time—861,459 votes. And he won in the Electoral College, 292 to 155. But under the Lodge plan Bryan would have defeated McKinley by an electoral vote of 218.8 to 214.4! See Table II on page 52. The elections of 1880 and 1896, although won by Garfield and McKinley with a majority of the popular vote, would also have been lost by those men under the Lodge-Gossett amendment.[21]

And if a clincher is needed, take the case of Wallace and Thurmond, both of whom got over a million votes in 1948, and who were within 13,000 of each other. Yet—under the Lodge plan, the latter would get 38 electoral votes, and the former only 10. (See Table I, supra, page 49.

These examples, of course, depend on the assumption that electoral votes will continue to be "cheaper," in terms of popular votes needed to secure one, in some states than in others. *Only* when the same number of popular votes is needed in all states for an electoral vote will the percentage of electoral votes be always fairly close to the popular vote. And this state of affairs will not, I think, exist in the foreseeable future.

It would seem unwise, then, to make this claim for the Lodge-Gossett bill.

2. To assert that certain voters are "disfranchised" when their candidates lose in the state is to make an appealingly plausible, but utterly illogical, statement.

TABLE II
Presidential Election of 1900

State	Popular vote in thousands Rep.	Dem.	Electoral vote present system Rep.	Dem.	Electoral vote Lodge-Gossett Rep.	Dem.
Alabama	55	96	......	11	3.4	7.4
Arizona	......	......	......	......	......	......
Arkansas	44	81	......	8	2.8	5.2
California	164	124	9	......	4.9	3.7
Colorado	93	122	......	4	1.7	2.3
Connecticut	102	74	6	......	3.4	2.5
Delaware	22	18	3	......	1.6	1.4
Florida	7	28	......	4	.7	2.9
Georgia	35	81	......	13	3.6	8.6
Idaho	27	29	......	3	1.4	1.6
Illinois	597	503	24	......	12.6	10.6
Indiana	336	309	15	......	7.5	6.1
Iowa	307	209	13	......	7.4	5.1
Kansas	185	162	10	......	5.2	4.6
Kentucky	226	234	......	13	6.2	6.7
Louisiana	14	53	......	8	1.6	6.4
Maine	65	36	6	......	3.7	2.3
Maryland	136	122	8	......	4.1	3.9
Massachusetts	239	157	15	......	8.6	5.6
Michigan	316	211	14	......	8.1	5.3
Minnesota	190	112	9	......	5.4	3.2
Mississippi	5	51	......	9	.8	8.1
Missouri	314	351	......	17	7.7	8.7
Montana	25	37	......	3	1.2	1.8
Nebraska	121	114	8	......	4.0	3.8
Nevada	3	6	......	3	1.0	2.0
New Hampshire	54	35	4	......	2.4	1.6
New Jersey	221	164	10	......	5.4	4.1
New Mexico	......	......	......	......	......	......
New York	822	678	36	......	19.1	15.5
North Carolina	133	157	......	11	5.0	6.0
North Dakota	35	20	3	......	1.8	1.2
Ohio	543	474	23	......	12.0	10.4
Oklahoma	......	......	......	......	......	......
Oregon	46	33	4	......	2.2	1.7
Pennsylvania	712	424	32	......	19.2	11.5
Rhode Island	33	19	4	......	2.4	1.5
South Carolina	3	47	......	9	.6	8.4
South Dakota	54	39	4	......	2.2	1.8
Tennessee	123	145	......	12	5.3	6.6
Texas	130	267	......	15	4.2	9.6
Utah	47	45	3	......	1.5	1.4
Vermont	43	13	4	......	3.0	1.0
Virginia	116	146	......	12	5.2	6.8
Washington	57	45	4	......	2.1	1.6
West Virginia	120	99	6	......	3.2	2.8
Wisconsin	266	159	12	......	7.2	4.3
Wyoming	14	10	3	......	1.8	1.2
TOTAL	7,220	6,358	292	155	214.5	218.8

Source: Senate Hearing on S. J. Res. 2, 81st Cong., p. 179.

No vote, in this republic, is lost (save by fraud) when cast, whether or not the candidate voted for wins. In another sense, all the votes cast for an individual are wasted if he loses, otherwise not. The Lodge-Gossett plan does no more than transfer the wasted vote from the state to the national level. It makes no more sense to say I was "disfranchised" by voting for Dewey in Georgia under the general ticket than it would to say I was "disfranchised" by voting for the losing candidate under the Lodge plan. It seems very clear that this claim must be utterly rejected: Basil Brewer said on this point, referring to Senator Lodge: "If the Senator were not so deadly serious about this matter, I would say he was joking."[22]

3. Senator Lodge's supporters say that his bill will enable the Republican party to invade the South, breaking it open for two-party action. It is unlikely that such G.O.P. votes will come from the tight Democratic majority in the South, which has every reason to remain "solid" under proportional allocation of electoral votes. There has not been the slightest tendency in the past for any kind of permanent Republican action. There is no basis for assuming that a strong G.O.P. minority would come into being as a result of his amendment, when that was not manifested when the South was "pressured as never before" by the civil rights controversy. It seems certain that more solid evidence can be adduced against this claim than has been presented for it. It therefore, I think, ought to be discounted.[23]

4. That elections will be "absolutely democratic," as Representative Gossett said[24] has already been demonstrated to be false. If democracy, or majority rule, is the ideal, then the Lodge-Gossett plan falls far short.

However, the rest of the claim is accurate. A choice

will be made by the voters in November—through the means of allowing a plurality election.

But to what will that lead? If a plurality vote elects a President, will there not be a strong tendency toward a multiparty system? One of the strongest forces preventing the permanent existence of any third party has been the hopelessness of electing a President when a majority of the electoral vote is required. Should new groups arise with a fair amount of popular strength, they will not be discouraged by the provisions of the Lodge-Gossett amendment, which would permit them to win with a much smaller number. Should a labor party be formed, as has been suggested in recent years, and should the South's 1948 break from the Democratic party not only become permanent but spread, there would be four parties, one of which might obtain the presidency with a quarter (or, in view of the earlier discussion, less) of the popular vote. Even if no new party became strong enough to capture the presidency, ". . . could [multiple parties] bid for a share in National Government power? . . . Today we have many bipartisan boards and commissions in the Federal Government. Might the new proposal send this into the direction of multipartisan boards with block pressure for concessions? Would not multiple parties, even if they failed to elect their Presidential candidate, be expected to elect members to Congress, and what effect would that have on Congressional organization?"[25]

Is this argument valid? Mr. Norman Thomas, in testifying before the House Committee, admitted: "In 1924 the Socialist Party . . . nominated the elder LaFollette, who was also nominated by a loose coalition known as Progressives. . . . I was very active in that campaign, and I am inclined to think that if, besides

54

getting about 5,000,000 popular votes, Mr. LaFollette had been able to get a proportionate electoral vote, that there would have been a better chance, rather than a less good chance, for a permanent organization of the party."[26]

The only American experience to which we can look for guidance in this regard is the practice of choosing governors and senators in some states, and municipal officers locally, on a plurality basis. Where this is done the result is invariably a multiplicity of parties and candidates—the more there are, the more are the votes for the leading candidates lowered. In most elections of this type (notably Texas) a run-off election has been the only answer. But no run-off provision is contained in this bill.[27]

In short: " 'Splinter' parties thrive on plurality voting systems where there is no defined percentage of total votes required for election and no provision for run-off. 'Splinter' parties cannot exist for long where a majority of all votes cast is required for election."[28]

It is known that the electoral system does not encourage a multiplicity of parties. It is known that proportional voting does encourage them. Whether the incentive of electoral votes will encourage them strongly or not cannot be categorically stated, but all the evidence available strongly indicates that the Lodge-Gossett plan would make for more—and weaker—parties.

It would be helpful to include here some remarks of Mr. Lucius Wilmerding, Jr., of Princeton, which deal with a rather abstract, but nevertheless vitally important, aspect of the question.

There would be . . . danger that [the proportional allotment provision of the Lodge bill] might give countenance to a move

55

for some form of proportional representation in our legislative bodies, national, state, and local. If the electoral vote of a state should be divided between the several parties in the same proportions as its popular vote, why not its representation in Congress also? Why should the votes of minorities in geographical constituencies be lost instead of combined with the votes of like minorities in other districts to make up mathematical constituencies or quotas? The answer I think is this. If a legislative body is to work, its mass must be men of moderate sentiments. . . . A member whose constituency is geographic must almost perforce be a moderate man; he must have regard for the opinions of the minorities within his district or risk defeat at the next election. But a member whose constituency is mathematical . . . must almost necessarily be immoderate; he must be wholly subservient to the wishes of his party managers, or of the splinter 'ism' which elects him, or risk being replaced at the next election by someone who is. . . .

.   .   .   .

I submit therefore that the danger to be apprehended from the adoption of proportional voting for the Presidency is real. It ought not to be ignored merely because the mode of choosing representatives is not dealt with in the amendment.[29]

5. Point five in the case for the Lodge-Gossett amendment is the most plausible of all. It describes the Electors as useless and dangerous, and calls for their elimination. It further criticizes the institution of a House election, and asks its elimination. Let us consider this point in two parts: first, the Electors. If I may draw again on the intellect of Mr. Wilmerding, I can do no better than to quote his statement in a recent article in the *Political Science Quarterly*, in which he weighed the advantages of retaining electors, even in the twentieth century, superbly:

Madison, first consulted on this subject in 1823, later made a very pertinent remark:

"One advantage of electors is, that altho' generally the

mere mouths of their Constituents, they may be intentionally left sometimes to their own judgment, guided by further information that may be acquired by them: and finally, what is of material importance, they will be able, when ascertaining, which may not be till a late hour, that the first choice of their constituents is utterly hopeless, to substitute in the electoral vote the name known to be their second choice."

There have been cases in which exactly this course was followed. In 1824, for example, the electors of North Carolina were pledged both to Jackson and Adams with the understanding that they would vote for the one who had the best chance of success. And as recently as 1912 the Roosevelt ticket of electors declared before election that, if Theodore Roosevelt could not become elected and it should become a contest between Taft and Wilson, they would vote for Taft.

Under the present arrangements this advantage of electors may be thought a small one. . . . But if the general ticket were to be broken up—either by the district system or by proportional voting—occasions might frequently arise when a majority opposition to a plurality candidate might make itself felt. On such occasions the advantage mentioned by Madison would be very considerable.

A second advantage of electors is that they act as a connecting link between the presidency and vice presidency. Being pledged to support the candidates of their parties for both offices, it can seldom happen that the popular election will result in the choice of a president of one party and a vice president of another. It is conceivable, however, that in a close election under the Lodge amendment a popular vice-presidential candidate of a minority party might succeed where his principal failed. The Twelfth Amendment to the Constitution, it will be remembered, was adopted precisely to prevent such a result.[30]

Turning to the assertion by adherents of the Lodge-Gossett amendment that the final decision in elections must be taken out of the House of Representatives, it is immediately apparent that the alternative being weighed in the balance with a House election is a plurality choice, as discussed above. Even if the evils attributed to a House election are valid, are they as

57

harmful to the nation as a multiparty system with a President chosen by a decided minority?[31] I think the answer must be no. More will be said on this subject in the next chapter.

6. The Lodge-Gossett plan would doubtless reduce the power of the larger states in the November election. It is to be questioned, however, whether the opposite effect might not be felt in the national conventions. The present representation of each state at both conventions is based upon the number of U.S. Representatives and Senators to which the state is entitled—this system being, of course, the thinnest of disguises for representation according to electoral strength—plus various bonuses for past victories for the party in question. A modified popular election scheme could well result in convention representation primarily based upon population, thus destroying at the primary stage as well as at the election stage that tendency toward equalization of strength provided by the Federal principle. More concretely, and as an example, as of the 1950 census Utah's population was about 4.7 per cent of New York's; Utah's electoral strength was about 9 per cent of New York's. Utah's delegate strength at the 1952 Republican national convention was (bonuses and all) about 14 per cent of New York's: something over its proportional electoral strength. If popular vote were used as the base, wouldn't Utah's delegation be about 7 per cent or 8 per cent of New York's (something over its proportional popular strength)? If so, the dominance of delegations and contenders from New York would be proportionately increased (it may be remembered that this possibility was feared by the members of the Constitutional Convention, though at the election stage since conventions had not yet been in-

vented). And in that event, wouldn't all the problems sought to be eliminated under point 6, page 45, *supra,* merely be referred back to—if not intensified at—the convention stage?

Because even party conventions must observe and follow political realities, this argument deserves serious thought.

During the course of this analysis it has become evident that most of the advantages claimed for the Lodge-Gossett plan would not materialize; on the contrary, it is more than probable that it might create a Frankenstein, in the shape of a multiparty, proportional representation system, in this country. In this opinion the U.S. Congress evidently shared, for while the Senate passed it by the required two-thirds vote on February 1, 1950, 64-27, the House of Representatives rejected it on July 17 of that year, 134 being in favor, and 210 against. Its supporters nevertheless continue to press for its submission to the states by Congress.

CHAPTER FOUR

In the first ten or eleven presidential elections, as mentioned earlier, there were three methods of choosing the Electors who in turn chose the President. The first, election by the state legislatures, died a natural, though gradual, death. No one has appeared to advocate a return to it since the Civil War. The second was the district method, and the third was the general ticket method. After the early years of the nineteenth century, when the Federalists attempted to maximize their votes by adopting the latter in several states,[1] the former was driven out of existence in much the same way as good money is driven out of circulation by bad. The general ticket method has reigned supreme from 1832 to the present.

It was with some dismay that several members of the Federal Convention watched the states settle on the general ticket plan, for it was the intention of the creators of the Electoral College to have its members chosen by districts in the states.[2] James Madison, one of the leaders of the group in the convention who plumped for the type of system eventually adopted, could hardly have been more explicit on the point: "The district mode was mostly, if not exclusively, in view when the Constitution was framed and adopted; and was exchanged for the general ticket and the legislative election as the only expedient for baffling the policy of the States which had set the example."[3]

Even though the Founding Fathers anticipated that the district system would be adopted it was, as a concession to states' rights, left to the legislature of each state to determine whether this or some other mode would prevail. Once the legislatures of some states seized upon the plan of delivering the entire electoral vote *en bloc* it became necessary for the politicians in other states to imitate that idea, in order to preserve their relative power in the selection of a President. And once the *en bloc* principle became universal, it was impossible for any state to revert to the original district plan.

Consequently the need to amend the Constitution was urged by those who were concerned about the preservation of the original political institutions of the national government. Only a measure binding upon all of the states and effective at the same time could remedy the situation. Walter Lippmann pointed out that if the district system in one state should attempt to compete with the general ticket in another, "The State which operates under a general ticket system will then exercise more weight in the electoral vote than it deserves. Therefore, the only way that the district system can be restored is by constitutional amendment which would prevent any State from adopting the general ticket system."[4]

Agitation to insure a uniform district system throughout the United States began as early as 1813. At that time a North Carolina representative introduced a plan which, in its final form, called for the creation of individual districts for each Elector in a state. During the following nine years similar resolutions were presented in nearly every Congress. Usually they were passed in one or the other of the

61

Houses by the required two-thirds vote, but were defeated in the other. In 1819 such a plan came the closest to success, being passed by the Senate 29-13, and defeated in the House 92-54 (not two thirds).[5]

In 1823 proposals were offered by Martin Van Buren of New York (the subsequent President) and Mahlon Dickerson of New Jersey. Both required the choice of Electors by districts, but Dickerson's plan further provided that in the event that the Electors made no choice, the Houses of Congress voting jointly, instead of the House alone voting by states, should choose the Chief Executive. Van Buren's plan provided that the Electors should be reassembled for a second balloting, in the event of no choice, with the election then reverting, if the second effort met with failure, to the House. These plans were not seriously considered.[6]

After the 1824 election, it was said that "There was no point on which the people of the United States were more perfectly united than upon the propriety, not to say indisputable necessity, of taking the election of President from the House of Representatives."[7] Therefore attempts to amend the Constitution centered around an effort to eliminate that provision. Most of the modes of election suggested included the district plan, with various devices to prevent a House election. As reported by one scholar, defenses at that time of the House election provision rested chiefly on the claim that any significant change would violate the principle of the Federal Compromise, as it was expressed in the clause of the Constitution forbidding the adoption of an amendment destroying state equality in the Senate.[8]

It is perhaps surprising to note that a much sounder defense was not employed. This defense rests on the structural organization of the United States. The legislature of the national government is constructed of the representatives of the citizens in the House, and the representatives of the states in the Senate. The Electoral College, as a means of choosing a President, was designed to be composed of the representatives of the first group, with the exception of the allotment of two Electors in each state to the second. When this method failed to select a President, the deciding factors were reversed in importance. This time the states had the chief voice, and yet the voters were not eliminated. This result was achieved by requiring the representatives of the people to vote by states for President. In sheer excellence of structural balance, and in high probability of reaching a definite and satisfactory choice, this plan has not been surpassed.[9]

In the 1870's, as was noted in the last chapter, attempts were made to return to the district system—but with a difference: the Electors were to be abolished (this was a feature of the plans of Senator Oliver P. Morton). Thus a compromise was offered between popular election and a system "conformable" to the original intent of the Constitution.

The district method of choosing Electors lay dormant thereafter as a possible constitutional amendment until the Eighty-first Congress. In 1949 G.O.P. Representative Frederic Coudert, Jr., of the seventeenth district of New York, introduced what has since come to be known as the Coudert plan (see Appendix A for the full text). It was produced by Representative Coudert in collaboration with Mr. J. Harvie Williams, a student of political science and chairman of the Citizens Political Committee in New York City. As an electoral reform proposal it occupied a back seat until the fate of the Lodge-Gossett plan became known toward the end of the Eighty-Second Congress. At the present time it is favored for extensive consideration, I was told by Mr. Williams, and has a good chance of receiving the support of both Houses of Congress.

In its present form, the Coudert amendment provides that presidential Electors, equal in number to the whole number of Representatives and Senators to which a state may be entitled, shall be elected in "the same manner" as are the Senators and Representatives. Thus the Electors would be chosen in Congressional districts, with the two Electors corresponding to the Senators chosen by the state at large. A further provision of the Coudert plan eliminates the House election by states in the event that the Electoral College fails to make a choice. Instead, the Houses of Congress would vote immediately in joint session, by the head, and the candidate receiving the highest tally on the respective roll calls for President and Vice-President would be declared duly elected.

It is the contention of Mr. Williams that

. . . the founding fathers regarded the electoral college as a *counterpart body* of the whole Congress. It was necessary then—and still is necessary now— to articulate the Federal and national features of our government in the election of a President as they are articulated in the two Houses of Congress, the Senate being a Federal body with equal representation for the States as units and the House of Representatives being a national body with representation based on the population of the States. Too, the electoral college was and is necessary to maintain the separation of executive and legislative power, an essential element in the structure of our National Government.[10]

Thus the Electoral College must be retained as an *alternative Congress*, so to speak, created to do the work which cannot be entrusted in the first instance to the legislative body. In order to be truly a counterpart body, however, it must be chosen in the same way as is the Congress. The advantage of this arrangement over an arbitrary districting plan will be noted below.

The supporters of the Coudert districting plan offer in its behalf the following points.

1. The electoral power of each state would be divided on the same basis as its Congressional power. This division would have two important consequences. First, the national parties would possess electoral power commensurate with their Congressional power—an ideal situation. It would be next to impossible to elect a President and a House of Representatives of differing parties. Second, the President and the whole Congress would have the same constituency cast up in the same form. Pressure groups and minority elements would have precisely the same influence in the choice of the President as they possess in the choice of the whole Congress. Thus the present basis of ideological conflict between the President and the Congress would be eliminated in favor of a wholesome affinity based on the closely similar political complexion of each department.[11]

This affinity of political thought between the President and the Congress which the Coudert amendment would tend to promote is not to be confused with a structural affinity. The Constitution provides for the separation and independence of the departments not because its authors were afraid that Congress and the President would *think alike*, but because they wished to minimize the possibility that the departments would *act together*. The checks and the antagonisms so skillfully fixed in the organization of the jurisdictions of the Congress and the President would remain to make difficult any such cooperative action for tyrannical purposes as the Founding Fathers feared.

2. The number of doubtful electoral votes in the largest states would be greatly reduced. Therefore the influence of the major states would fall to a more proportionately equitable level. Most of the consequences of the domination of the large states in the presidential elections which were discussed in the last chapter would disappear. Principal among these are (1) the vastly exaggerated importance of small, yet pivotal, minorities in these states, and (2) the almost exclusive reliance of the major parties upon candidates from the large states.[12]

3. The choice of a President in the event that no election is made by the Electoral College is made by the original body (Congress) immediately. The present system violates the Republican principle of numerical equality and the Federal principle which qualifies the numerical equality with state equality.[13] The Coudert plan would substitute a method of election which would preserve for the smaller states their present advantage as expressed in the Electoral College, while alloting them no greater power. Prolonged deadlock and resultant intrigue is prevented by the provision that a choice shall be made on the first ballot.

4. Accidents will no longer affect the national scene in disproportionate ways. Local issues, bringing out a high percentage of voters, or bad weather, reducing the number materially, will not affect the electoral vote of an entire state. In the districts, too, results will probably be close to those expected under normal conditions—for those conditions which are abnormal will influence the members of all parties in the area equally.

In the same way the importance of local fraud will be reduced.

5. The district method

... would be agreeable to the rights of individuals: for, in entering into society, and submitting to be bound by the decisions of the majority, each individual retained the right of voting for himself wherever it was practicable, and of being governed by a majority of the vicinage, and not by majorities brought from remote sections to overwhelm him with their accumulated numbers. It would be agreeable to the interests of all parts of the States; for each State may have different interests in different parts; one part may be agricultural, another manufacturing, another commercial; and it would be unjust that the strongest should govern, or that two should combine and sacrifice the third. The district system would be agreeable to our present Constitution, which, in giving to each Elector a separate vote, instead of giving to each State a consolidated vote, composed of all its electoral suffrages, clearly intended that each mass of persons entitled to one Elector, should have the right of giving one vote, according to their own sense of their own interests.[14]

Several arguments have been brought to bear against the district system. Those who feel that the general ticket system "disfranchises" the voter on the losing side statewise, of course complain of the same effect in the case of districts: the losing voter does not have an elector to represent him. This argument has been dealt with in the preceeding chapter; it will be sufficient to say here that the voter is not less "disfranchised" by being on the losing side in the election of a Congressman!

There is objection that the district system will obliterate state lines.[15] To a certain extent this argument is true. The sharp division of states in a presidential election will be certainly lessened. It is, however, I think, a superficial viewpoint which sees the splitting of electoral votes within the state as destructive of the Federal nature of the presidency. The Electors are the same in number as under the general ticket system. The *state's* Electors, two in number, will continue to be chosen on a general ticket basis, and unquestionably they will be decisive in a number of elections. The remainder of the Electors are popular, e.g., they are allotted on the national, rather than the Federal basis. On that account they have been wrongly diverted to a Federal-type election system, and should be restored to their original functions. State lines will not, then, be obliterated: they will be reduced to the importance intended by the framers of the Constitution.

By all odds the most important charge which has been made against the district system is its liability to gerrymandering, and it is a charge which is impossible to answer fully. Indeed, as one student of the problem says, "... no plan has yet been devised that can prevent the reapportionment of districts to suit the needs of partisanship or eradicate the instinct of the politician to use all means not forbidden by statute to secure an election triumph."[16] Yet the effects of gerrymandering can be minimized. That the House of Representatives changes from party to party indicates that although some districts can be successfully gerrymandered, a sufficient number are not to permit the party which is popularly successful to assume control.

Madison, the statesman who advocated the district system, urged that an anti-gerrymandering provision be enacted by Congress (which has[17] the power to govern the casting of electoral votes) in order to prevent the sudden alteration of districts before election time.[18] Even if such a measure were not entirely successful, "At the very worst it could result in the choice

68

of a man who was considered by the second largest group of persons in the country as best fitted for the office. . . . If the electoral districts were gerrymandered on the same plan as the congressional districts . . . the result of the election would be to produce a president in political sympathy with the majority of the House of Representatives."[19] It is Mr. Wilmerding's conclusion that the district system is vastly preferable, even though subject to possible gerrymandering, to both the general ticket system and the Lodge-Gossett proposal of proportional allotment of electoral votes.[20]

Criticism of the plan to permit a joint session of Congress to choose the President when he is not elected by the Electors is entirely lacking (except on the part of those who wish to substitute a plurality election—which was discussed in Chapter Three). It is assumed by nearly all students of the problem that a House election is iniquitous and evil—nowhere is there any proof that there is a reason why this must be so. The election of 1824 is usually pointed to with horror. Yet what is the basis of this horror? The fact that the candidate with a popular plurality was not elected? If so, for what reason does the Constitution provide that a choice of the *three* top candidates, electorally, shall be voted upon by the House? Surely, so that the best, or else the best compromise, candidate can be chosen.[21]

The Coudert amendment provides that the eventual election, if necessary, will be in the Congress in joint session, and that the candidate with the most votes on the first ballot will be chosen. I would suggest that this provision is at best completely useless, and at worst, dangerous. If the Electors are chosen in the same manner as the new Congress, will not the Congressional vote very closely approximate the electoral total? The only difference will be in the votes of the previously elected Senators whose political affiliations differ from the presently chosen Federal Electors—probably insignificant in number. Thus it is clear that a joint session election under these circumstances would be no election at all—rather merely a confirmation of the candidate with the highest electoral vote. It can be, in fact, said to be a type of plurality election in disguised form. The dangers of plurality elections were discussed in Chapter Three; there is no need to do more than suggest here the probable encouragement of splinter parties, with the consequent chaos.

The defense of a House election by states set forth on pages 62-63 seems to hold up structurally and rationally. In the absence of a reasoned counterargument (for which I have searched long and in vain), or even of an acceptable substitute, the principles which governed the adoption of that system by the Federal Convention must, I think, hold good today.

CHAPTER FIVE

The first two chapters of this work traced and analyzed the creation of the Electoral College and its historical development. The following chapters dealt with the two major trends in proposed reforms of the institution. This chapter will draw together the threads of 160 years of experience and of the thoughts of many minds in an attempt to reach a conclusion which is both feasible and correct in principle.[1]

The question can best be summarized and considered in two parts. The first is the concrete query "How should the President be elected?" and the second will deal with alternate or eventual methods of choice if a President cannot always be chosen by the method which provides the answer to that query.

The present method of selecting a President is through Electors chosen in each state by a plurality vote of the qualified citizens—the general ticket. It has no discernible advantages over the district system of choosing Electors (discussed below). It possesses, on the other hand, a number of disadvantages. It discourages the development of opposition parties in states in which one party is constantly predominant. In "close" states it increases the reward for fraudulent manipulation of elections. It promotes the domination of the largest states over a presidential election, which in turn exaggerates the power and influence of splinter groups and pressure groups within those states. It denies the national principle in presidential elections, which asks that each geographically compact mass of persons be supplied with a representative, in favor of the Federal principle, which supplies the states with a specific amount of representation as states.

Legislative election of the Chief Executive in the first instance has not been advocated since the Constitutional Convention abandoned the idea.[2] It was then found to be subject to several serious drawbacks, chief among which was the probable interdependence of the President and Congress, resulting in the domination of one by the other. Also, the Founding Fathers saw that intrigue would unquestionably be present and corruption would probably be present in an election by a body whose members represented loosely organized groups.

Popular election, the choice without regard to state lines of a President by a majority or plurality of those who choose to vote in a given election, would cure some of the evils of the general ticket system. It would not, however, materially diminish the domination of the populous states, and it goes to the other extreme in suppressing the Federal principle in favor of the national principle. In addition, it possesses very serious disadvantages in its own right. First, such a method of election would tend to reduce voting requirements to the lowest common denominator throughout the nation. Political necessity would dictate that each state cast as many ballots as possible, so that if one state, for example, reduced the voting age to sixteen years, all the others would be obliged to follow suit in order to preserve their relative power positions. Second, it would withdraw from each state the right to participate in a presidential election according to population, substituting participation according to competitive voting strength in each election. There would be substituted for a stable relationship an unstable one, with no compensating advantage.[3] Third, a multiparty system with its instability and kaleidoscopic shifts in party alignments would certainly develop. Of course, it is unlikely that an amendment proposing this change would receive the support of the smaller states in the Union or under the circumstances the approbation of all Congressmen from the larger states. These reasons make it clear that a popular election is not to be preferred to the general ticket system.

Proportional division of the electoral votes of each state in accordance with the popular vote received by each candidate is a distinct improvement over a popular election, in that it disposes of two of the objections mentioned above. It further does not contain most of the faults of the general ticket system. However, it makes hash of the Federal-national principle, in that the electoral power granted to the state is twisted out of recognition and the electoral power given to each geographic mass of people is given to each mathematical mass of people. As a result, it would foster the principle of proportional representation throughout the national government, for, if each mathematical mass is entitled to be represented in one election, it certainly is entitled to the same in other elections. In addition, splinter parties would be encouraged by the possibility of securing the presidency without a majority of the electoral vote, and by the certainty of securing representation in Congress by mathematical means when the proportional representation principle is extended. It is a basic tenet of a republican form of government that it shall be able to act; if there is a multiplicity of parties, whether their representatives are seated by PR or not, action will be discouraged. By requiring a minimum of electoral votes for election (such as the arbitrary figure of 40 per cent) the encouragement to new parties would be only minimized, not eliminated. In view of the inherent dangers in this plan I am convinced that to adopt it would be a step fatal to the type of government we now enjoy. The faults of even the general ticket system are less important than those of this proposal.

The election of Electors by Congressional districts, with the two state Electors chosen in the same way as the Senators, is a method of choosing a President free from every defect mentioned in connection with the general ticket system, legislative election, popular election, and proportionate representation. It would encourage, as much as any technical device can, the development of the two-party system in one-party states; it would reduce the premium for fraud in "close" states; it would reduce the disproportionate influence of the large states and minimize the influence of local pressure groups and factions; and it agrees with the principles on which the government is founded by relating correctly the Federal and the national elements of power in a presidential election. Its chief positive merit lies in correspondence of political sympathy which it would create between the President and Congress, tending to eliminate the ideological conflict between the President and Congress which has been fostered by the general ticket system. It possesses none of the destructiveness inherent in the PR system. Because a majority of the electoral vote is required, and because the Electors and Congressmen would continue to be elected on a geographical rather than a mathe-

74

matical basis, it would not encourage permanent splinter parties. The obstacles placed in the path of even temporary minority parties would be only slightly less strong under the district system than under the general ticket system.

The sole objection to the district plan which carries weight is its liability to gerrymandering. Inasmuch as Congress has the power to regulate the election of U.S. Representatives (and has used it—as in 1911), if a district plan whose wording specified that the Electors should be chosen "in the same way" as Representatives should become part of the Constitution, the Congress could without additional authority provide certain anti-gerrymandering statutes. To be effective, such statutes would need to specify that the districts should be compact in nature and as uniform in population as possible, and that the districts might not be altered save after the (ten year) reapportionment. It is likely with the presidency at stake that these provisions would be enforced sufficiently to keep gerrymandered districts at the minimum possible in a two-party government. In any case, this disadvantage is not worse than the corresponding one under the general ticket system: at present, fraud in New York state could cost one party forty-seven electoral votes, while the quasi-legal fraud of gerrymandering probably would cost less. Finally, that party control of the House of Representatives shifts at the present time in accordance with the expressed desire of the qualified voters indicates that even now gerrymandering is not so extensive as to maintain the unbroken power of one party.

The Constitution, then, ought to be amended to provide for the choosing of presidential Electors in the same way as are Representatives and Senators. Sections One and Two of the Coudert amendment accomplish this purpose, and they should be adopted.

The district method of election, however, will not always elect a President, since a majority of Electors appointed are required, as now, to elect. There must, therefore be a means to make a choice when the Electoral College fails. The two alternatives which are feasible seem to be the present system—a House election by states—and the method proposed by Representative Coudert. The latter calls for a vote, by head, in the two Houses of Congress assembled in joint session. The leading candidate on the first roll call would be elected.

This method would be useless at best and dangerous at worst. It would be useless because the membership of the Congress would be very close indeed in political sympathy to the membership of the Electoral College which, after all, is one of the aims of the district system. As a result, the vote in Congress would be a virtual rubber stamp of the electoral vote. And, because the candidate who possessed an electoral plurality would invariably be elected President, the method would be dangerous. It amounts to a virtual negation of the provision that a majority of the electoral vote is necessary to win. It would be a disguised plurality election. And all of the evils which follow upon plurality elections—many parties and an ineffective, compromising government—would appear at Washington.

Even if the wording of this provision were changed to require a majority of the joint session for election, it would possess a serious drawback. The first ballot would still echo the Electoral College. After that ballot, a number of Congressmen would be required to change their votes in order to effect an election. Whence would these turncoats come, doomed thereafter politically as they doubtless would be? On most occasions the needed number might be small, but if only once the vote were split fairly evenly, between three or four candidates, the mechanism—and the government—would break down. Even with the additional requirement of a majority to elect the method remains sufficiently tricky to merit only rejection.

The present system is not defective in these respects. It is the converse of a choice by Electors. When the Electoral College, in which the national principle is predominant, fails to elect, the House election by states, in which the Federal principle is predominant, does so. It will usually provide a choice immediately, the composition of Congress by states nearly always differing sharply from the composition by head. The election of 1824 illustrates this fact. When it does not choose immediately, only a very few men need usually change their votes to produce a result. The election of 1800 illustrates this fact. And above all, the House election by states preserves the essential principle of majority election.

On this account I submit that the language of the Twelfth Amendment with regard to a House election should be retained in force. The Senate should be kept as the agency to choose a Vice President so that, if the House ever should fail to elect, a legitimate head of the government will be available on January 20.

In reviewing the merits of the various plans to amend the Constitution with respect to the election of the President the value of Electors as individuals was ignored. Is it possible, and is it wise, to attempt to restore to the members of the Electoral College some of the function of independent thinking and action assigned to them by the Federal Convention?

Madison was quoted earlier to the effect that Electors might, when the first choice of their constituents was hopelessly lost, cast their ballots for their second choice. "... if the general ticket were to be broken up—either by the district system or by proportional voting—occasions might frequently arise when a majority opposition to a plurality candidate might make itself felt. On such occasions the advantage mentioned by Madison would be very considerable."[4] This amount of independence is certainly the very minimum to be expected from Electors.

Beyond that, one scholar claims, "To try to restore the electoral scheme of the fathers would be a chimerical undertaking. To attempt the creation of any plan in conflict with the plain trend of institutional development would be equally unwise."[5] For the Electors to regain a measure of their original purpose would not, however, be necessarily in conflict with party developments, nor would the undertaking of that restoration be certainly doomed. John Holcombe, writing in the *Forum* at approximately the same time said, "In no reactionary spirit, therefore, but with views thoroughly progressive, the writer urges a return for relief to the wisdom of the fathers by making effective their admirable device—the Electoral College."[6] His plan for "making effective" the Electoral College would prohibit party nominating conventions and call for a meeting of the Electors in convention for a choice of candidates, after which the members would return to their states to cast their ballots. No constitutional amendment would be necessary to effectuate this plan.

Any revival of the Electoral College as a body to

choose a President, influenced but not governed by the desires of the qualified voters, will await a general recognition of the desirability of such an institution. Adoption of the district system may increase the probability of such a development, and it was with this possibility in mind that I became fully and firmly convinced that the district system should and will be adopted into the Constitution.

APPENDIX A

*Original Provision of the U.S. Constitution Respecting the
Election of the President*

Article II, Section 1

Each State shall appoint, in such manner as the Legislature thereof may direct, a Number of Electors, equal to the whole Number of Senators and Representatives to which the State may be entitled in the Congress: but no Senator or Representative, or Person holding an Office of Trust or Profit under the United States, shall be appointed an Elector.

(The Electors shall meet in their respective States, and vote by Ballot for two persons, of whom one at least shall not be an inhabitant of the same State with themselves. And they shall make a List of all the Persons voted for, and of the Number of Votes for each; which List they shall sign and certify, and transmit sealed to the Seat of the Government of the United States, directed to the President of the Senate. The President of the Senate shall, in the Presence of the Senate and House of Representatives, open all the Certificates, and the Votes shall then be counted. The Person having the greatest Number of Votes shall be the President; if such Number be a Majority of the whole Number of Electors appointed; and if there be more than one who have such Majority, and have an equal Number of Votes, then the House of Representatives shall immediately chuse by Ballot one of them for President; and if no Person have a Majority, then from the five highest on the List the House shall in like manner chuse the President. But in chusing the President, the Votes shall be taken by States, the Representation from each State having one Vote; A quorum for this Purpose shall consist of a Member or Members from two-thirds of the States, and a Majority of all the States shall be necessary to a Choice. In every Case, after the Choice of the President, the Person having the greatest Number of Votes of the Electors shall be the Vice President. But if there should remain two or more who have equal Votes, the Senate shall chuse from them by Ballot the Vice President.)

—the text enclosed in parentheses was superseded by the Twelfth Amendment to the Constitution, adopted on September 25, 1804. Source: Norton, *The Constitution of the United States*, pages 275-6.

Article Twelve of the Constitution, adopted in 1804 and still in effect

The Electors shall meet in their respective states and vote by ballot for President and Vice-President, one of whom, at least, shall not be an inhabitant of the same state with themselves; they shall name in their ballots the person voted for as President, and in distinct ballots the persons voted for as Vice-President, and they shall make distinct lists of all the persons voted for as President and of all persons voted for as Vice-President, and of the number of votes for each, which lists they shall sign and certify, and transmit sealed to the seat of the government of the United States, directed to the President of the Senate;—

The President of the Senate shall, in the presence of the Senate and House of Representatives, open all the certificates and the votes shall then be counted;—

The person having the greatest number of votes for President shall be the President, if such number be a majority of the whole number of Electors appointed; and if no person have such majority, then from the persons having the highest numbers not exceeding three on the list of those voted for as President, the House of Representatives shall choose immediately, by ballot, the President. But in choosing the President the votes shall be taken by states, the representation from each state having one vote; a quorum for this purpose shall consist of a member or members from two-thirds of the states, and a majority of all the states shall be necessary to a choice. And if the House of Representatives shall not choose a President whenever the right of choice shall devolve upon them, before the fourth day of March next following, then the Vice-President shall act as President, as in the case of the death or other constitutional disability of the President. The person having the greatest number of votes as Vice-President, shall be the Vice-President, if such number be a majority of the whole number of Electors appointed, and if no person have a majority, then from the two highest numbers on the list, the Senate shall choose the Vice-President; a quorum for the purpose shall consist of two-thirds of the whole number of Senators, and a majority of the whole number shall be necessary to a choice. But no person constitutionally ineligible to the office of President shall be eligible to that of Vice-President of the United States.

—Source: Norton, *op. cit.*, page 281.

The proposed Lodge-Gossett Amendment to the Constitution
(S.J. Res. 2, 81st Cong. 1st sess.)

SECTION 1. The executive power shall be vested in a President of the United States of America. He shall hold his office during the term of four years, and together with the Vice President, chosen for the same term, be selected as provided in this Constitution.

The electoral college system of electing the President and Vice President of the United States is hereby abolished. The President and Vice President shall be elected by the people of the several States. The electors in each State shall have the qualifications requisite for electors of the most numerous branch of the State legislature. Congress shall determine the time of such election, which shall be the same throughout the United States. Until otherwise determined by the Congress, such election shall be held on the Tuesday next after the first Monday in November of the year preceeding the year in which the regular term of the President is to begin. Each State shall be entitled to a number of electoral votes equal to the whole number of Senators and Representatives to which such State may be entitled in the Congress.

81

Within forty-five days after such election, or at such time as the Congress shall direct, the official custodian of the election returns of each State shall make distinct lists of all persons for whom votes were cast for President and the number of votes cast for each, and the total vote of the electors of the State for all persons for President, which lists he shall sign and certify and transmit sealed to the seat of the Government of the United States, directed to the President of the Senate. The President of the Senate shall in the presence of the Senate and House of Representatives open all certificates and the votes shall then be counted. Each person for whom votes were cast for President in each State shall be credited with such proportion of the electoral votes thereof as he received of the total vote of the electors therein for President. In making the computations, fractional numbers less than one one-thousandth shall be disregarded unless a more detailed calculation would change the result of the election. The person having the greatest number of electoral votes for President shall be President. If two or more persons shall have an equal and the highest number of such votes, then the one for whom the greatest number of popular votes were cast shall be President.

The Vice President shall be likewise elected, at the same time and in the same manner and subject to the same provisions, as the President, but no person constitutionally ineligible for the office of President shall be eligible to that of Vice President of the United States.

SECTION 2. Paragraphs 1, 2, and 3 of section 1, article II, of the Constitution and the twelfth article of amendment to the Constitution, are hereby repealed.

SECTION 3. This article shall take effect on the tenth day of February following its ratification.

SECTION 4. This article shall be inoperative unless it shall have been ratified as an amendment to the Constitution by the legislatures of three-fourths of the States within seven years from the date of its submission to the States by the Congress.

—Source: *Hearings before a Subcommittee of the Committee on the Judiciary*, etc., U.S. Senate, Eighty-First Congress, First Session, (#89804) pages 1 and 2.

The Proposed Coudert Amendment to the Constitution
(H.J. Res. 11, 82nd Cong., 1st sess.)

SECTION 1. Each State shall choose a number of electors of the President and Vice President, equal to the whole number of Senators and Representatives to which the State may be entitled in the Congress, in the same manner as its Senators and Representatives are chosen. But no Senator or Representative or person holding an office of trust or profit under the United States shall be chosen elector.

SECTION 2. The electors shall meet in their respective States, and vote by ballot for President and Vice President, one of whom, at least, shall not be an inhabitant of the same state with themselves; they shall name in their ballots the person voted for as President, and in distinct ballots the person voted for as Vice President; and they shall make distinct list of all persons voted for as President, and of all persons voted for as Vice President, and of the number of votes for each, which list they shall sign and certify, and transmit sealed to the seat of government of the United States, directed to the President of the Senate; the President of the Senate shall, in the presence of the Senate and the House of Representatives, open all the certificates and the votes shall then be counted; the person having the greatest number of votes for President shall be the President and the person having the greatest number of votes for Vice President shall be the Vice President, if such numbers be majorities of the whole number of electors chosen.

SECTION 3. If no persons voted for as President or Vice President have a majority of the whole number of electors chosen, then from the persons having the highest numbers, not exceeding three, on the lists of those voted for as President and Vice President, the Senate and House of Representatives, assembled and voting as one body, shall choose immediately the President, and then the Vice President, or either, as the case may be; a quorum for these purposes shall consist of three-fourths of the whole number of Senators and Representatives, and the persons receiving the greatest number of votes for President and for Vice President on the respective roll calls shall be the President and Vice President. But no person ineligible to the office of President shall be eligible to the office of Vice President.

—Source: a copy of the bill introduced by the Hon. Frederic Coudert, Jr., on Jan. 3, 1951.

APPENDIX B

Notes to Chapter One

1. James Wilson, quoted on page 164, Farrand, *The Framing of the Constitution of the United States.*
2. James Madison, *The Journal of the Federal Convention*, p. 90.
3. *Ibid.*, p. 91.
4. *Ibid.*, pp. 136-38.
5. *Ibid.*, pp. 365-69. (paraphrased)
6. *Ibid.*, p. 369.
7. *Ibid.*, p. 387.
8. *Ibid.*, pp. 387-91.
9. *Ibid.*, pp. 427-30.
10. *Ibid.*, pp. 434-36.
11. *Ibid.*, pp. 600-603.
12. *Ibid.*, pp. 644-45.
13. *Ibid.*, p. 432.
14. *Ibid.*, p. 659.
15. Madison in *The Federalist Papers*, as quoted by Sterling Edmunds, *Struggle for Freedom*, p. 130.
16. Farrand, *op. cit.*, p. 175.

Notes to Chapter Two

1. McKnight, *The Electoral System of the United States*, p. 28.
2. O'Niel, *The American Electoral System*, p. 32.
3. Stanwood, *A History of Presidential Elections*, p. 11.
4. *Ibid.*, p. 24.
5. One time many of them did deserves mention. In 1872 the Democratic candidate, Horace Greeley, died after the election in which he was defeated, but before the Electors cast their ballots. The Electors were faced with the awesome choice of casting their ballots for a dead man or selecting a meritorious individual.
6. Dougherty, *The Electoral System of the United States*, p. 252.
7. *Ibid.*, p. 32.
8. With one exception: a Rhode Island Federalist Elector foresightedly cast a vote for John Jay, in order that Adams and Pinckney might not be tied for the chief office.
9. Dougherty, *op. cit.*, p. 234.
10. The statistics were taken from Stanwood, *A History of the Presidency*, pp. 163-64.
11. O'Niel, *op. cit.*, p. 56.

12. Stanwood, *A History of Presidential Elections*, p. 63.

13. *Ibid.*, p. 118. With one exception: Michigan in 1892.

14. *Ibid.*, p. 79.

15. *Ibid.*, p. 116.

16. *Loc. cit.*

17. This strategem reminds one of the efforts of the Thurmond candidacy in 1948 to bring about a House election—which came closer than anyone had thought to success. A mere handful of votes redistributed in key states would have accomplished Thurmond's aim.

18. *The Gallup Political Almanac for 1948*, p. 32, and Stanwood, *A History of Presidential Elections*, p. 234 for the Lincoln statistics.

19. O'Niel, *op. cit.*, p. 166.

20. Stanwood, *A History of the Presidency*, p. 380.

21. *Loc. cit.*

22. Field, *The Electoral Votes of 1876.*

23. *Proceedings of the College of Presidential Electors of the State of New York*, p. 13.

24. Stanwood,*A History of Presidential Elections*, p. 239.

25. McKnight, *op. cit.*, pp. 199-200.

26. *Ibid.*, p. 207. But there exists doubt that the Supreme Court could enforce its judgement; see Dougherty, *op. cit.*, p. 92.

27. Dougherty, *op. cit.*, supports this view on p. 96.

Notes to Chapter Three

1. Sayles (Ed.), *The Constitutions of the State of Texas with . . . the Constitution of the Confederate States*, pp. 288-90.

2. The quotation is from Dougherty, *op. cit.*, p. 327. The other material on Benton is from *Ibid.*, pp. 326-27, and from O'Niel, *op. cit.*, pp. 321-23.

3. Dougherty, *op. cit.*, p. 334.

4. As quoted in O'Niel, *op. cit.*, p. 254.

5. *Ibid.*, p. 338.

6. Dougherty, *op. cit.*, p. 349.

7. Stanwood, *A History of Presidential Elections*, pp. 345-48, and Dougherty, *op. cit.*, pp. 344-55.

8. Dougherty, *op. cit.*, pp. 355-63; Stanwood, *A History of Presidential Elections*, pp. 349-50.

9. The hearings referred to are: *Hearings before Subcommittee No.1 of the Committee on the Judiciary, House of Representatives, on Proposing an Amendment to the Constitution Providing for the Election of President and Vice President*, 81st Congress, First Session; and *Hearings before a Subcommittee of the Committee on the Judiciary, United States Senate, on a Joint Resolution proposing an Amendment to the Constitution of the United States Providing for the Election of President and Vice-President*, 81st Congress, First Session. In subsequent notes these hearings will be designated, for the sake of brevity, as *House Hearing* and *Senate Hearing*.

10. From a letter to Senator Lodge, page 8 of a booklet by Senator Henry Cabot Lodge entitled *The Electoral "College" vs. The Will of the People*. And from a statement by Senator Lodge, *Senate Hearing*, p. 84.

11. *House Hearing*, p. 27.

12. Senator Lodge, *Senate Hearing*, p. 4.

13. *House Hearing*, p. 12; quote from Mr. Lea, p. 37.
14. *Ibid.*, pp. 10-20 (Representative Gossett).
15. *Ibid.*, pp. 15-16.
16. *Ibid.*, p. 18.
17. *Ibid.*, pp. 16-18.
18. *Ibid.*, p. 16.
19. Wilmerding, "Reform of the Electoral System," *The Political Science Quarterly*, March, 1949, pp. 1-2 of the reprint edition of Robert Dresser of Providence, Rhode Island.
20. *Senate Hearing*, p. 141 (Basil Brewer).
21. *House Hearing*, pp. 83-84 (Representative Case).
22. The quotation is from *Senate Hearing*, p. 142; the body of the remarks is paraphrased and enlarged from p. 57.
23. *Ibid.*, pp. 59, 68-69.
24. *House Hearing*, p. 12.
25. *Senate Hearing*, p. 53 (Senator Ferguson).
26. *Ibid.*, p. 169.
27. *Ibid.*, p. 138.
28. *Loc. cit.*
29. Wilmerding, *op. cit.*, pp. 7-8.
30. *Ibid.*, pp. 16-17.
31. On February 1, 1950, when the Senate voted on the Lodge-Gossett proposal, an amendment was offered and adopted by voice vote to the effect that a candidate, to be elected, must receive 40 per cent of the electoral vote. Failing this, the Houses of Congress in joint session, by majority vote, would choose immediately the President. At best, this development represents an unsatisfactory compromise between majority and plurality election. *The Congressional Record*, Feb. 1, 1950, p. 1304 (unbound).

Notes to Chapter Four

1. O'Niel, *op. cit.*, pp. 97-98.
2. Dougherty, *op. cit.*, p. 292.
3. In a letter to George Hay, in 1823, as quoted by Dougherty, *op. cit.*, p. 330.
4. From a column in the *New York Herald Tribune* of March 7, 1950, as reprinted in *The Congressional Record* of March 22, 1950, p. A2222 of the unbound edition.
5. The material in this paragraph was derived from Stanwood, *A History of Presidential Elections*, pp. 74-76.
6. Dougherty, *op. cit.*, p. 328.
7. Martin Van Buren, as quoted by Dougherty, *op. cit.*, p. 253.
8. O'Niel, *op. cit.*, p. 252.
9. Suggested by a conversation with Rose Wilder Lane, novelist and political analyst.
10. From a letter of J. Harvie Williams to Representative Coudert, reproduced on p. A1860 of *The Congressional Record* for March 8, 1950. Italics added.
11. Suggested by Mr. William's remarks, as printed in *The Congressional Record* of March 8, 1950, pp. A1860-61.
12. *Loc. cit.*

13. Wilmerding, *op. cit.*, p. 19.

14. Senator Benton—speaking in 1824—as quoted by Wilmerding, *op. cit.*, p. 9.

15. Dougherty, *op. cit.*, p. 372.

16. *Ibid.*, p. 367.

17. Wilmerding, *op. cit.*, p. 12.

18. Dougherty, *op. cit.*, p. 331.

19. Wilmerding, *op. cit.*, p. 13.

20. *Loc. cit.*

21. A House election, which was at that time expected by many, might in 1860 have averted the war between the states. See O'Niel, *op. cit.*, p. 166.

Notes to Chapter Five

1. The material in this chapter is not extensively footnoted since it has been derived from the preceding chapters.

2. For the purpose of this work, it is assumed that an amendment changing the mode of electing the President would be presented and adopted by itself, not connected with far-reaching changes in other departments of the national government. I cannot consider here the merits and demerits of the parliamentary type of government presently advocated by Henry Hazlitt and others.

3. *House Hearing*, p. 68 (Representative Lea).

4. Wilmerding, *op. cit.*, p. 17. Supposing that a Huey Long appeared and captured a plurality of the electoral vote, it would be highly probable that the Republican and Democratic electors would combine forces against him.

5. Dougherty, *op. cit.*, p. 390.

6. Reprinted by the U.S. Senate, 62nd Congress, 3rd session, document No. 1092.

BIBLIOGRAPHY

American Institute of Public Opinion (compiler), *The Gallup Political Almanac for 1948*, published by the compiler, Princeton, 1948.

Anonymous, *The Constitution of the United States of America; The Proximate Causes of its Adoption and Ratification*, J. & G. S. Gideon, Washington, D.C., 1846.

BEAN, LOUIS, *How to Predict Elections*, Knopf, New York, 1948.

The Congressional Record, March 8, 1950 (unbound), pages A1859-A1861, extension of remarks by Hon. Frederic Coudert, Jr.

The Congressional Record, March 16, 1950, (unbound), page A2079, extension of remarks by Hon. Frederic Coudert, Jr.

The Congressional Record, March 22, 1950, (unbound), pages A2221-A2223, and page A2228, extensions of remarks by Hon. Frederic Coudert, Jr.

DOUGHERTY, J. H., *The Electoral System of the United States*, G. P. Putnam's Sons, New York, 1906.

EDMUNDS, STERLING, *Struggle for Freedom*, Bruce Publishing Co., Milwaukee, 1946.

FARRAND, MAX, *The Framing of the Constitution of the United States*, Yale University Press, New Haven, 1913.

FIELD, DAVID D., *The Electoral Votes of 1876*, Appleton & Co., New York, 1877.

GRAF, WILLIAM (Ed.), *Statistics of the Presidential and Congressional Election of November 7, 1944*, U.S. Government Printing Office, Washington, 1945.

Hearing before the Committee on Election of President, Vice President and Representatives in Congress, published by U.S. House of Representatives, 71st Congress, 2nd session, 1930 (#107487).

Hearing before the Committee on Election of President, Vice President and Representatives in Congress, published by U.S. House of Representatives, 72nd Congress, 1st session, 1932 (#107531).

Hearings before the Committee on Election of President, Vice President and Representatives in Congress, published by the U.S. House of Representatives, 71st Congress, 2nd session, 1930 (#107486).

Hearings before Subcommittee Number One of the Committee on the Judiciary, Proposing an Amendment to the Constitution of The United States Providing for the Election of President and Vice President, published by U.S. House of Representatives, 80th Congress, 1st session, 1947 (#64509).

Hearings before Subcommittee Number One of the Committee on the Judiciary, Proposing an Amendment to the Constitution of the United States Providing for the Election of President and Vice President, published by the U.S. House of Representatives, 81st Congress, 1st session, 1949 (#87711).

Hearings before a Subcommittee of the Judiciary: A Joint Resolution Proposing an Amendment to the Constitution of the United States Providing for the Election of President and Vice President, published by the U.S. Senate, 81st Congress, 1st session, 1949 (#89804).

HOLCOMBE, J. W., *The Electoral College*, published by the U.S. Senate, 62nd Congress, 3rd session, document number 1092; 1913.

Journal, Acts and Proceedings of the Convention which Formed the Constitution of the United States, published by Thomas B. Wait, Boston, 1819.

LODGE, H. C., *The Electoral "College" vs. The Will of the People*, U.S. Government Printing Office, Washington, 1948.

MADISON, JAMES, *Journal of the Federal Convention*, Albert, Scott & Co., Chicago, 1894. 2 volumes.

MCKNIGHT, DAVID, *The Electoral System of the United States*, Lippincott & Co., Philadelphia, 1878.

NORTON, THOMAS J., *The Constitution of the United States*, America's Future, Inc., New York, 1946.

O'NIEL, CHARLES, *The American Electoral System*, G. P. Putnam's Sons, New York, 1887.

PATERSON, ISABEL, *The God of the Machine*, Putnam, New York, 1943.

Presidential Elections: Provisions of the Constitution and the United States Code, Department of State publication 2177.

Proceedings of the College of Presidential Electors of the State of New York, published by the College, Albany, 1877.

READ, CONYERS (Ed.), *The Constitution Reconsidered*, Columbia University Press, New York, 1938.

SAYLES, J. (Ed.), *The Constitutions of the State of Texas, with the Reconstruction Acts of Congress, The Constitution of the Confederate States, and of the United States*, Gilbert Book Co., St. Louis, 1888.

STANWOOD, EDWARD, *A History of the Presidency from 1788 to 1897*, Houghton Mifflin Co., Boston, 1912.

STANWOOD, EDWARD, *A History of Presidential Elections*, Osgood & Company, Boston, 1884.

WILMERDING, LUCIUS, "Reform of the Electoral System," the *Political Science Quarterly*, March 1949, as reprinted by Robert Dresser, Providence, June, 1949.

8170